D1567887

Breast Cancer

Titles in the Diseases and Disorders series include:

Acne
ADHD
Alcoholism
Allergies
Amnesia
Anorexia and Bulimia
Anxiety Disorders
Asperger's Syndrome
Autism
Blindness
Brain Trauma
Brain Tumors
Cancer
Cerebral Palsy
Cervical Cancer
Childhood Obesity
Dementia
Depression
Diabetes
Epilepsy
Hepatitis

Human Papillomavirus (HPV)
Infectious Mononucleosis
Malnutrition
Mental Retardation
Migraines
MRSA
Multiple Sclerosis
Personality Disorders
Phobias
Plague
Post Traumatic Stress
  Disorder
Prostate Cancer
Sexually Transmitted
  Diseases
Skin Cancer
Speech Disorders
Sports Injuries
Sudden Infant Death
  Syndrome
Thyroid Disorders

DISEASES & DISORDERS

Breast Cancer

Lizabeth Hardman

LUCENT BOOKS
A part of Gale, Cengage Learning

GALE
CENGAGE Learning

Detroit • New York • San Francisco • New Haven, Conn • Waterville, Maine • London

© 2010 Gale, Cengage Learning

Every effort has been made to trace the owners of copyrighted material.

LIBRARY OF CONGRESS CATALOGING-IN-PUBLICATION DATA

Hardman, Lizabeth.
  Breast cancer / by Lizabeth Hardman.
    p. cm. -- (Diseases & disorders)
  Includes bibliographical references and index.
  ISBN 978-1-4205-0279-4 (hardcover)
  1. Breast--Cancer. I. Title.
  RC280.B8H366 2010
  616.99'449--dc22

                                                        2009053705

Lucent Books
27500 Drake Rd
Farmington Hills MI 48331

ISBN-13: 978-1-4205-0279-4
ISBN-10: 1-4205-0279-4

Printed in the United States of America
 2 3 4 5 6 7 14 13 12 11 10

Printed by Bang Printing, Brainerd, MN, 2nd Ptg., 11/2010

Table of Contents

"The Most Difficult Puzzles Ever Devised"

Charles Best, one of the pioneers in the search for a cure for diabetes, once explained what it is about medical research that intrigued him so. "It's not just the gratification of knowing one is helping people," he confided, "although that probably is a more heroic and selfless motivation. Those feelings may enter in, but truly, what I find best is the feeling of going toe to toe with nature, of trying to solve the most difficult puzzles ever devised. The answers are there somewhere, those keys that will solve the puzzle and make the patient well. But how will those keys be found?"

Since the dawn of civilization, nothing has so puzzled people—and often frightened them, as well—as the onset of illness in a body or mind that had seemed healthy before. A seizure, the inability of a heart to pump, the sudden deterioration of muscle tone in a small child—being unable to reverse such conditions or even to understand why they occur was unspeakably frustrating to healers. Even before there were names for such conditions, even before they were understood at all, each was a reminder of how complex the human body was, and how vulnerable.

While our grappling with understanding diseases has been frustrating at times, it has also provided some of humankind's most heroic accomplishments. Alexander Fleming's accidental discovery in 1928, of a mold that could be turned into penicillin has resulted in the saving of untold millions of lives. The isolation of the enzyme insulin has reversed what was once a death sentence for anyone with diabetes. There have been great strides in combating conditions for which there is not yet a cure, too. Medicines can help AIDS patients live longer, diagnostic tools such as mammography and ultrasounds can help doctors find tumors while they are treatable, and laser surgery techniques have made the most intricate, minute operations routine.

This "toe-to-toe" competition with diseases and disorders is even more remarkable when seen in a historical continuum. An astonishing amount of progress has been made in a very short time. Just two hundred years ago, the existence of germs as a cause of some diseases was unknown. In fact, it was less than 150 years ago that a British surgeon named Joseph Lister had difficulty persuading his fellow doctors that washing their hands before delivering a baby might increase the chances of a healthy delivery (especially if they had just attended to a diseased patient)!

Each book in Lucent's Diseases and Disorders series explores a disease or disorder and the knowledge that has been accumulated (or discarded) by doctors through the years. Each book also examines the tools used for pinpointing a diagnosis, as well as the various means that are used to treat or cure a disease. Finally, new ideas are presented—techniques or medicines that may be on the horizon.

Frustration and disappointment are still part of medicine, for not every disease or condition can be cured or prevented. But the limitations of knowledge are being pushed outward constantly; the "most difficult puzzles ever devised" are finding challengers every day.

A Sisterhood of Struggle and Strength

Christa was a healthy twenty-nine-year-old when, during a routine physical, the nurse practitioner examining her found a lump in her right breast. Because of her age, the nurse felt it was probably just a cyst, but nevertheless, she encouraged Christa to see a doctor. The doctor took a biopsy—a small piece of the lump—and had it examined under a microscope. When the doctor's office called her in to get the results a day earlier than she planned, she tried not to worry. "I am still confident that it's nothing," writes Christa in her blog. "That is probably why they called me in early right? I go in to the exam room and wait for Dr. Fuller. He comes in and tells me it's cancer. I think my brain shuts down. He's going on and on about the treatments and the surgery that I would need. I'm not really hearing what he is saying; I'm just focusing on not crying. I go out to the main office, thankful that it is empty. He's trying to schedule a mammogram [an X-ray of the breast] and a blood test. I hear him on the phone saying, 'she's only 29, and can you get her in soon?'"[1]

Christa's case was somewhat unusual. Although breast cancer is the second most commonly diagnosed cancer in women in the United States after skin cancers, most breast cancers occur in women over the age of fifty. The National Cancer Institute estimated that by the end of 2009, approximately 192,370 cases of breast cancer would be diagnosed in women in the United States, and that over 40,000 of them would die from it. They also estimated that more than 1,900 men would develop breast cancer, with about 440 deaths.

African American and Hispanic women are less likely to get breast cancer, but their death rates are higher after diagnosis, possibly because of genetic differences in the tumors, barriers to getting effective health care, or getting diagnosed at a later stage of the disease. Women who are of Ashkenazi Jewish descent have a higher risk of breast cancer, because they tend to carry and pass on an important genetic mutation that increases breast cancer risk. Asian and Native American women have a lower incidence and death rate than Caucasian and African American women, although these occurrences have been increasing over the last two decades.

The overall incidence of breast cancer, however, has been declining since 2002, and death rates from the disease have been decreasing since 1990. Thanks to greatly improved understanding of the nature of breast cancer and improved treatment methods, as of 2008, there are about 2.5 million women in the United States who have survived breast cancer.

A Long History

Breast cancer is one of the oldest known forms of cancer in humans. The Edwin Smith Papyrus, an Egyptian text that dates back to about 1600 B.C., mentions eight cases of tumors, or masses, of the breast and states that there was no treatment for it. It was not until the seventeenth century, when doctors learned of the relationship between cancer and the lymphatic system through which cancer spreads, that treatment methods began to develop. Eighteenth century surgeons in France and Scotland were among the first to treat breast cancer with a mastectomy—the surgical removal of the breast—along with

Breast cancer is one of the oldest forms of cancer known to man as proven the Edwin Smith Medical Papyrus, an Egyptian text that dates back to about 1600 B.C. The document mentions about eight cases of breast tumors.

the chest wall muscle underneath it and the lymph nodes in the axilla, or armpit.

Renowned American surgeon William Halsted began performing mastectomies in 1882. His radical procedure often involved removing both breasts, along with the chest muscles and axillary lymph nodes on both sides. The procedure commonly left the woman disabled and in a great deal of pain, and there was no medical or scientific evidence that the procedure actually resulted in a higher cure rate. Despite these drawbacks, the procedure remained in use even into the 1980s. As one woman put it, after her radical mastectomy in 1971, "I went to the hospital feeling perfectly healthy, and came out grotesquely mutilated—a mental and physical wreck."[2]

In the late 1970s, with a more complete understanding of breast cancer and how it spreads, surgeries were developed that spared the chest wall muscles and often the lymph nodes in the armpit. A radical mastectomy became less common in favor of the tissue-sparing lumpectomy, which removes only the part of the breast that contains the cancer. "That particular advance is an enormous benefit because of the improved quality of life and improved self-image," says Dr. Lawrence Solin, a professor in radiation oncology at the University of Pennsylvania School of Medicine. "There are better outcomes all the way around."[3]

Coping with Fear

Despite these drastic improvements in breast cancer detection and treatment, a diagnosis of breast cancer can still be cause for a great deal of fear and anxiety. Until the middle of the twentieth century, cancer was not openly discussed. "Cancer was a word that was whispered," writes Betty Ford, wife of former President Gerald Ford, whose breast cancer was diagnosed in 1974. "If somebody had cancer, and particularly breast cancer, it was a topic that people covered up and only whispered about behind their hand so no one would hear it."[4]

Lack of knowledge about cancer meant that a diagnosis of the disease would almost certainly result in death, and people feared cancer above all other diseases. Because breast cancer is almost exclusively a disease of women, and because doctors and patients often felt uncomfortable talking about a woman's breasts, many women delayed seeking medical attention, even when the cancer was far advanced. Many people considered

Awareness of breast cancer began to be raised as more high-profile women, such as First Lady Betty Ford, publicly announed that they had been diagnosed with the disease.

it to be the woman's own fault if she got breast cancer—that women who lived pure and healthy lives would not get such a "shameful" disease.

Since the 1970s, however, attitudes about discussing breasts have become much more open. High-profile women, such as Ford, actresses Shirley Temple and Jill Eikenberry, Supreme Court Justice Sandra Day O'Connor, and WNBA player Edna Campbell took their struggles with breast cancer public, which increased awareness of breast cancer and diminished the negative assumptions about the women who got it. As Ford writes, "It was a real awakening for the women of the United States to have the wife of the president have breast cancer and speak of it…People were shocked and yet they became more open about addressing the issue."[5]

Since that time, women have become much more comfortable talking about their own bodies. Also, having more women in the medical profession means that women with a hesitancy to see a male doctor, can choose a female doctor instead. This feeling of comfort may encourage women to seek medical attention sooner. "I remember when you couldn't even say 'breast', let alone 'breast cancer,'" says Fran Visco, president of the National Breast Cancer Coalition. "That has changed quite a bit. Even if you have breast cancer, you are still full of life."[6] Dr. Solin adds, "There has been enormous improvement in our ability to detect it early, and treat and cure patients. We have had a dramatic reduction in mortality, and the treatments are more effective."[7] Increased awareness of women's health issues, coupled with medical advances, has provided women with options for treatment to actively fight the disease with a realistic hope for survival.

CHAPTER ONE

What Is Breast Cancer?

All the parts of the human body—bones, muscles, blood, organs, and skin—are made up of cells. Cells are like highly specialized building blocks; liver cells build a liver, heart cells build a heart, skin cells build the skin. In a normal, healthy body, microscopic structures called genes, located in the nucleus, or center, of each cell, regulate the creation, growth, and death of each kind of cell. Normally, as the cells age and die off—a process called apoptosis—they are replaced with new cells in an orderly, controlled fashion. When damage occurs, such as when a person gets a cut in the skin, the genes instruct the cells involved to grow faster to replace the damaged tissue. When the damage is healed, the genes tell the cells to slow down and return to their normal rate of growth.

Sometimes, the normal genetic mechanism that tells cells when to stop growing malfunctions because of errors, or mutations, in the genes, and normal apoptosis does not take place. Nurse practitioner Rosalind Benedet explains, "Unlike normal cells, which divide a limited number of times before they die, these mutated cells have become 'immortal'—they never stop dividing. One cell divides into two, two divide into four, and so on, and this mass of cells forms a tumor."[8] A tumor is a lump, or mass, of abnormal cells.

Some tumors are harmless. They grow to a certain size and then usually stop growing, and they tend to grow in only one

How a Normal Cell Becomes Cancer

Normally, human cells grow, divide, and die off in a controlled fashion. This process is controlled by the DNA in the nucleus of the cell—the genetic material that provides all the instructions to the cell about what its function is and how it is supposed to behave.

Damage to the DNA of a cell causes errors, or mutations, in the DNA, which causes the cell to malfunction. Normally, cells either repair the damage, or they die. If enough mutations occur in the DNA because of the damage, however, the cell may lose its ability to repair itself and also lose the ability to die off. Instead, it may begin to grow and divide out of control, creating more and more cells with the damaged DNA instructions. Cancer cells never mature into the kind of tissue they were supposed to become, they do not stay in one place, and they do not respond to instructions from other cells.

Damage to DNA is most often caused by something the person is exposed to in the environment. People can help minimize their chances of getting cancer by avoiding carcinogens—things that are known to damage DNA and cause cancer. Common carcinogens include: tobacco in all its forms; ultraviolet radiation (from sun exposure or tanning beds); toxic industrial chemicals such as pesticides, vinyl chloride, and asbestos; and some viruses, including the human papilloma virus.

place. These harmless tumors are referred to as benign tumors. A lipoma, made of fat cells, is an example of a benign tumor which grows under the skin. A fibroma is a benign tumor that can show up in any part of the body. Skin tags and keloid scars are examples of skin fibromas. Some benign tumors can grow very large and may cause discomfort if they press on internal organs or nerves. They may be unsightly if they grow on a vis-

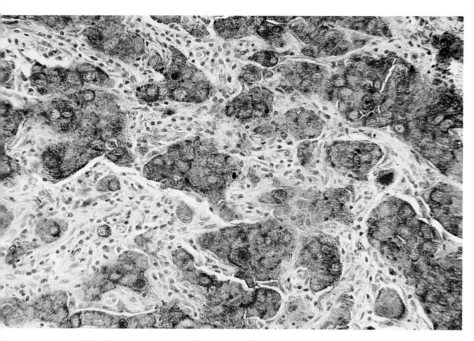

A slide showing magnification of cancer cells in the breast tissue. Cancerous tumor cells can be especially harmful when they leave the part of the body where they began growing and spread to other parts of the body.

ible part of the body. If a benign tumor creates problems for the person who has it, it can usually be surgically removed, with no harm done. Benign tumors are not cancer.

What is Cancer?

A cancer is also an abnormal growth of cells in a particular organ or tissue type, but unlike benign tumors, cancerous tumors are potentially harmful to the individual that has one. There are several different classes of cancer types. Breast cancer is one of the classes called carcinomas. Cancerous tumors are malignant, and unlike benign tumors, they do not stop growing. Another important difference is that cancerous tumor cells can leave the part of the body where they begin and spread to other parts of the body. Once there, the cells can grow and create new tumors. When cancer cells migrate to another part of the body and start to grow there, the process is called metastasis. A cancer that spreads to another organ is referred to by the organ from which it started. For example, breast cancer which has spread to the bones is called metastatic breast cancer, not bone cancer. Cancers that metastasize to another body organ can devastate the body, alter treatment plans, and may even result in death.

How Does Cancer Cause Death?

There are several ways that cancer can cause the death of the person who has it. If the cancer is located inside a vital organ, it can interfere with the function of that organ. For example, a brain tumor can grow large enough that it presses on delicate brain tissue, leading to coma and eventual death. A tumor in the lung can block air passages and cause respiratory failure.

Most cancer deaths, however, are not caused by the primary, or main, tumor. They are caused when cells from the primary tumor metastasize to other organs and grow there. A common example is colon cancer. Colon cancer by itself does not usually cause death, but when it spreads, it tends to spread to the liver, a vital organ. Eventually, the colon cancer cells replace so much liver tissue that the patient dies from liver failure. Breast cancer most commonly spreads to the lungs, liver, brain, and bones.

Another way that cancer causes death is through tumor burden, which is related to the amount of tumor tissue containing cancerous cells in the body. The rapid growth and multiplication of cancer cells requires a great deal of energy. Cancer cells take for themselves much of the body's energy sources and proteins that are needed for building healthy tissues. They do this by actually creating their own blood vessels, a process called angiogenesis. In addition, cancers tend to produce large amounts of chemicals called cytokines. Cytokines are normally produced in small amounts in areas of injury, but the abnormal amounts produced by cancers severely disrupt the body's normal physiological functions. These two characteristics of cancer cells are what cause many cancer patients to lose a lot of weight, become very weak, and look as if they are "wasting away"—a condition called cachexia. The more the cancer spreads, the higher the tumor burden becomes, and the more cachectic the patient becomes. As the patient weakens, his body becomes unable to combat even minor infections. Death comes from illnesses such as pneumonia—an infection of the lungs or sepsis—an infection in the blood. Tumor burden is the most common way in which breast cancer causes death.

Anatomy of the Breast

The human breast is a gland. Glands are organs that produce and secrete substances needed by the body. For example, sweat glands secrete sweat. The pancreas secretes insulin for metabolizing sugar. The breast secretes milk for feeding infants. The breast is made up mostly of fatty tissue and breast tissue. These tissues are what give the breast its size and shape, depending mostly on genetic factors. Nerves, small veins, and small arteries run through the breast. Everything is held together with tissue called connective tissue. The breast has no muscle of its own (except for some very tiny muscles around the nipple), but

A side and front illustration of the breast showing the various parts that make up the gland.

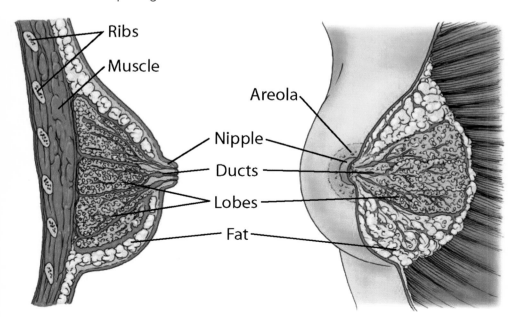

right behind the breast and in front of the ribs is the pectoralis muscle, the main muscle of the chest.

Breast tissue is made up of a system of lobules and ducts. Lobules are clusters of very small sacs that look like tiny grapes. They are lined with special cells that produce milk. Each breast has about twelve to fifteen lobules. Ducts are tiny tubes that carry the milk from the lobules out of the breast through the nipple during breast feeding. Ducts from the lobules join together into larger ducts, eventually ending in about five to ten ducts that end at the nipple. Around the nipple is a circular pigmented area called the areola. The areola secretes small amounts of fluid during breast feeding to help keep the nipple lubricated.

Also running through the breast are tiny vessels called lymphatic vessels. They carry a clear fluid called lymph that filters out bacteria and waste products of cell metabolism as well as any other foreign substances that may get into the bloodstream. Lymph also contains immune system cells, such as white blood cells that help fight off infections. Lymphatic vessels lead to lymph nodes—small bean-shaped structures that are part of the immune system. Lymph nodes collect and concentrate the unwanted materials in the lymph so that immune system cells can eliminate them from the body.

Lymph nodes are found throughout the body, but chains or clusters of lymph nodes are especially numerous in the neck, the axilla (armpit), and groin area. When breast cancer spreads, it is most commonly by way of the lymphatic vessels. Breast cancer cells can enter the lymphatic vessels and travel to the lymph nodes. From there, they can get into the bloodstream and travel to other parts of the body.

The Breast and Cancer

Breast cancers may be described in one of two main ways, depending on the part of the breast in which they begin. The first type is called lobular carcinoma. As its name suggests, lobular carcinomas arise in the lobules—the parts of the breast that produce milk. About 15 percent of breast cancers are lobular carcinomas. The more common type is ductal carcinoma. Ductal carcinomas arise in the ducts. They account for about 85 percent of breast cancers.

Another important distinction to make concerns whether or not the cancer has spread outside the breast. Breast cancer that has not yet spread is called carcinoma in situ. The term "in situ" means "in place." These are cancers which have not yet left the lobules or the ducts where they began. Although they are called carcinomas, these tumors have not yet developed the ability to actually leave the breast. For this reason, carcinoma in situ is often considered a "pre-cancerous," or noninvasive, condition. A woman may have ductal carcinoma in situ (DCIS) or lobular carcinoma in situ (LCIS). DCIS is the most common form of noninvasive breast cancer, and almost all women with this kind can be cured. LCIS is not actually a true cancer because it does not grow through the wall of the lobules, but women with LCIS do have an increased risk of developing the more serious invasive carcinoma.

Invasive, or infiltrating, carcinoma is a cancer that has already spread outside of the duct or lobule and into the surrounding breast tissue. Once in the breast tissue, it can leave the breast via the lymphatic vessels and nodes and metastasize to other organs. Eighty percent of all invasive breast cancers are invasive ductal carcinoma (IDC), 10 percent are invasive lobular carcinoma (ILC), and the rest are other types of breast cancer.

Other Types of Breast Cancer

Besides these four more common forms of breast cancer, there are several other, less common types. One example is medullary carcinoma, a form of IDC that gets its name from its color, which is similar to tissue in the brain called the medulla. It represents only about 3 to 5 percent of all breast cancers. Its cells are very large, and medullary tumors are very distinctive from the normal breast tissue around them. It is somewhat fast-growing but does not tend to spread to the lymph nodes as quickly as other invasive forms of breast cancer. Medullary carcinoma can usually be treated successfully.

Another less common type of breast cancer is inflammatory breast cancer (IBC). IBC is a very serious and aggressive form of breast cancer, but it is even less common than medullary carcinoma, accounting for about only 1 to 3 percent of breast cancers. It tends to affect younger women more than other types do. It first shows up with swelling, redness, pain, and warmth in the breast. The skin begins to look thick and bumpy, like the skin of an orange. This sign is called peau d'orange, which is French for "orange skin." Inflammatory breast cancer may be hard to diagnosis at first because it is so uncommon, it does not show up well on X-rays, and because the symptoms are so similar to an infection of the breast called mastitis. Inflammatory breast cancer may be suspected if the symptoms do not respond to antibiotics and if there is no fever present.

A third example is Paget's disease of the nipple, which accounts for 2 to 5 percent of all breast cancers. In almost all cases of Paget's disease, the woman already has another form of breast cancer, such as DCIS or IDC. The cause of Paget's disease is not clear, but one theory is that certain cancer cells, called Paget cells, break off from the main tumor and move through the milk ducts to the skin of the nipple and areola. Because the early symptoms are minor—redness, itching, and some flaking of the skin, it is often undiagnosed until the underlying cancer is found.

Staging Breast Cancer

After the type of breast cancer has been determined, a further way to describe and classify it is by its stage. "Patience is important here, for both the woman and her physician," caution cancer specialists Dr. Yashar Hirshaut and Dr. Peter I. Pressman. "The reason a precise identification is important is that these are the factors that affect risk and that make it possible to determine what ought to be done to treat the patient most effectively."[9] Staging also helps doctors and their patients get a better idea of the prognosis—how well the patient is likely to respond to the treatment methods and what the most likely outcome of treatment will be. It also provides a standard-ized way for breast cancers to be described so that treatment results and outcomes can be shared with other physicians, and

An illustration of a cross-section of a cancerous breast which shows an invasive tumor, light blue in color, towards the bottom of the breast. This cancer would be considered at least Stage I cancer because of its invasive nature.

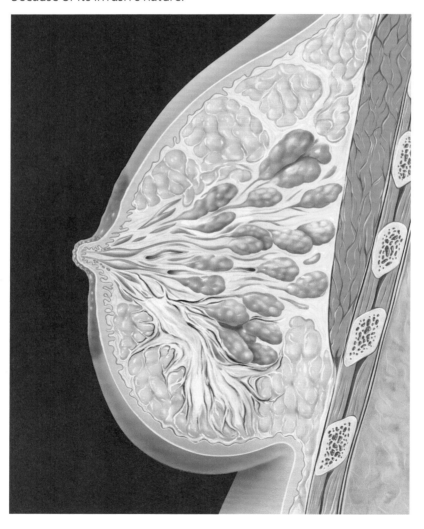

so that physicians and researchers everywhere can have consistent understanding when it comes to studying and learning about breast cancer.

The stage of a breast cancer depends on its size, its location in the breast, whether it is invasive or noninvasive, whether or not lymph nodes are involved, and whether or not it has spread to other organs. Stage 0 is a noninvasive DCIS or LCIS, which has not spread outside of the duct or lobule. Stage I is an invasive cancer that has spread outside the duct or lobule, but has not spread to the lymph nodes and is less than 2 centimeters in size.

Stage II cancers are further divided into IIA and IIB. Stage IIA describes tumors in which cancer cells have spread to the lymph nodes in the armpit, or there are no cancer cells in the nodes but the tumor is between 2 and 5 centimeters in size. Stage IIB means that the tumor is between 2 and 5 centimeters and has spread to the lymph nodes, or that the tumor has not yet spread to the nodes but is larger than 5 centimeters in size.

Stage III is divided into three substages labeled IIIA, IIIB, and IIIC. In Stage III cancers, the tumor may be larger than 5 centimeters in size. The axillary nodes are positive for cancer cells, and they have begun to clump together or stick to other structures in the axilla. There may also be cancer cells in the nodes near the breastbone, or it may have spread to other areas of the chest wall or to the skin of the breast.

In Stage IV breast cancer, the cancer has metastasized to other organs in the body. Sometimes, the breast tumor is not found before it metastasizes, and the diagnosis of breast cancer comes later, when the metastatic tumor causes symptoms in the other part of the body.

Survival Rates for Breast Cancer

Staging breast cancer is very important because it helps doctors to provide information to the patient about her prognosis. When cancer doctors talk about treatment, they often speak in terms of "five year survival rate." This term refers to the percentage of people with a given type of cancer who are still living at least five years after diagnosis of the cancer. Survival rates for different kinds of cancer are determined based on the experiences of thousands of other people who have been diagnosed with the same kind of cancer at the same stage. Statistics about survival rates cannot predict what will happen to an individual patient, however, because each person's situation—the stage of their cancer, other health problems, access to medical care, and many other factors—is unique to that particular patient.

Survival rates vary depending on the type of cancer involved and, more importantly, the stage at which it is diagnosed. Generally speaking, the earlier the cancer is diagnosed and treated, the better the survival rate. According to the American Cancer Society, for most breast cancers, those which are at Stage 0 or I when diagnosed have a survival rate of 100 percent. This means that out of 100 women diagnosed at Stage 0 or Stage I, all of them can expect to be living at least five years after diagnosis. Stage II cancers have an approximately 86 percent five year survival. Stage III cancers have about 57 percent survival, and survival for Stage IV is about 20 percent. An exception to this is inflammatory breast cancer (IBC). Because IBC is very aggressive and is more likely to have metastasized by the time it is diagnosed, IBC is almost always staged at Stage IIIB or IV at the time of diagnosis. The five year survival rate for IBC is only about 25 to 40 percent.

Risk Factors for Breast Cancer

It is not fully understood what makes cancer start in some people and not others, but there are several risk factors that may make it more likely that a person will develop breast cancer. The most important are gender and age. Both men and women have breast tissue, but women are approximately 100 times more likely than men to get breast cancer. This is partly because they just have more breast tissue, but more importantly, women produce much more of the female hormone estrogen, which is known to support the growth of some kinds of breast cancer.

The risk of breast cancer increases with age. As people grow older, the normal wear and tear of aging can cause genes to

Breast Cancer in Men

Both boys and girls have some breast tissue in childhood, but when boys reach puberty, increased levels of the male hormone testosterone, along with decreased levels of the female hormone estrogen, prevent development of any significant amount of breast tissue. They may have a few underdeveloped ducts, but, essentially, they have no lobules in their breasts. Because of this, breast cancer in men is usually ductal carcinoma.

The National Cancer Institute estimates that as many as nineteen hundred men will get breast cancer in 2009. "Even though we don't think of men as having breasts, they have breast tissue and are susceptible to getting breast cancer," says Dr. Sharon Giordano of the M.D. Anderson Cancer Institute in Dallas, Texas. "All men have some degree of residual breast tissue behind the nipples. It may be very small, but just like any part of the body can get cancer, that part of the body can get cancer."

Men who have a genetic condition called Kleinfelter's syndrome are at increased risk for getting breast cancer because men with this condition produce more estrogen than other men. Men with BRCA-1 or BRCA-2 mutations are also at increased risk for developing breast cancer by age seventy. There is a 1 percent risk for men with BRCA-1 and a 6 percent risk with men with BRCA-2. As with women, other risk factors for male breast cancer include obesity, smoking, and alcoholism.

Quote from Madison Park, "Original KISS drummer celebrates surviving breast cancer." CNN.com, 2008. http://www.cnn.com/2009/HEALTH/10/15/male.breast.cancer/index.html.

mutate, which can affect the normal process of apoptosis. Genetic abnormalities that occur because of the normal aging process are responsible for 90 percent of breast cancers. Most advanced cases of breast cancer—about two out of three—are seen in women over the age of fifty-five. About 10 percent are caused by genetic mutations inherited from a parent.

Inherited Risk

Genetic mutations can occur because of aging, but they can also be inherited, or passed down, from parent to child. About 20 to 30 percent of women with breast cancer have a first-degree relative—a mother, sister, or daughter—who has been diagnosed with it. The risk is higher if the relative was diagnosed before age forty.

An illustration of chromosome 13 showing the BRCA-2 gene. Women who have this gene are 60 percent more likely to get breast cancer sometime in their lives and are more likely to develop the disease before the age of fifty.

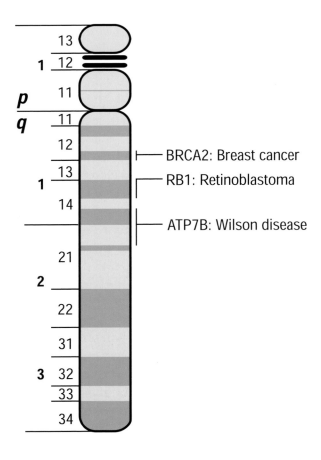

Chromosome 13

The most common inherited mutations are called BRCA-1 and BRCA-2 (for BReast CAncer), discovered in 1994. Normal BRCA genes work by making proteins that fix mutations in other genes. Cells with abnormal BRCA genes cannot fix mutations, including those in another gene called PTEN. PTEN is a tumor suppression gene. It makes cancer cells stop growing. Dr. Ramon Parsons of Columbia University Medical Center explains what happens when there is a BRAC mutation: "If a cut occurs in PTEN, there is no way for the cell to fix it. It is like cutting the brake on a cable car. If PTEN is broken, you turn on a pathway that tells the cells to grow. It tells the cell to start dividing. It tells the cell, 'don't die.'"[10] Abnormal BRCA genes are unable to fix mutated PTEN, so it cannot stop tumor cell growth. Women with mutations in the BRCA genes have about a 60 percent chance of getting breast cancer at some time in their lives, and they are more likely to develop it earlier—under age fifty.

Health History and Breast Cancer

Women who start their menstrual periods early in life—before age twelve—or stop having periods late—after age fifty— are also at a higher risk of developing breast cancer. This is because they are exposed to more estrogen (a hormone that is commonly found in higher amounts in women) over their lifetimes, which has been linked to increased risk of breast cancer. Women who do not have children, or who had their first child after age thirty, are also at higher risk because early pregnancy causes changes in breast tissue that seem to help protect it from becoming cancerous.

Women with a previous diagnosis of breast cancer have a three to four times higher risk of developing a new cancer in the other breast or in another part of the same breast. Women who have had radiation treatment for other kinds of cancer also have a higher risk, especially if the radiation was given during adolescence, when the breast tissue was developing. Women who, in the 1940s through the 1960s, received a synthetic form of estrogen called DES to help prevent miscarriage may have an increased risk, and their female children may also have a slightly increased risk.

Controllable Risk Factors

Gender, age, and heredity are risk factors for breast cancer that a person has no control over. There are other risk factors, however, that can be controlled. Rosy Daniel, author of *The Cancer Prevention Book*, believes that controllable risk factors are of paramount importance…. "just like heart disease," she says, "cancer is primarily a lifestyle-related disease. This means that if we change our lifestyle and habits, we can considerably reduce our risk of getting cancer."[11]

There is evidence that alcohol consumption may increase the risk of getting cancer. According to a very large study done from 1996 to 2001, in the United Kingdom, called the Million Women Study, even small amounts of daily alcohol consumption increased the risk of several kinds of cancer, but the biggest increase in risk was related to breast cancer. The study found that for every 10 grams (about ⅓ ounce or 10cc) of alcohol

Studies have shown that drinking even small amounts of alcholic beverages on a daily basis can increase a woman's risk of developing breast cancer.

consumed per day, the risk of developing breast cancer went up by 12 percent, regardless of the type of alcohol consumed. Another study, published in 2009, found that women who have fourteen or more alcoholic drinks, of any kind, per week are 24 percent more likely to get breast cancer compared to women who do not drink. The reason for the increased risk is not yet clear, but researchers think it may be related to alcohol's effect on the way the body metabolizes estrogen.

Other lifestyle choices that may affect breast cancer risk include smoking, diet, weight, and physical activity. Smoking increases risk of many kinds of cancer because the many toxins in cigarette smoke damage the genetic material inside the cells. A diet that is high in cholesterol and fat, especially animal fats, is associated with increased risk of several types of cancer, including breast cancer. Eating a lot of red meats and processed meats such as bacon and sausage may contribute to this risk because they may contain hormones, pesticides, or antibiotics that can damage cells. Obesity, especially later in life, is also associated with greater risk of breast cancer, because fat is the main source of the hormone estrogen after menopause, the time in a woman's life when her ovaries stop producing it. Regular physical activity, especially in young adulthood, can help decrease risk of breast cancer because it helps to keep body weight under control.

Hormone Replacement and Breast Cancer

During and after menopause, a woman may experience unpleasant symptoms such as hot flashes, mood swings, night sweats, and weight gain. Many women choose to treat these symptoms with hormone replacement therapy (HRT), to replace the hormones that her body no longer produces. There are two main kinds of HRT. One form uses estrogen alone. Estrogen alone, however, increases the risk of uterine cancer. Adding the hormone progesterone decreases that risk. Women who have had a hysterectomy (surgical removal of the uterus) are usually given estrogen alone. Women who still have their uterus are usually given the estrogen/progesterone combination. There is a higher risk of breast cancer associated with the combination form of HRT, but the risk decreases back to zero within five years of stopping the combined HRT. Estrogen replacement by itself does not seem to increase the risk of breast cancer, although some studies have shown some increased risk if it is used for more than ten years.

Breast tissue is very sensitive to these kinds of controllable risk factors. They may all trigger that first cell to become a cancer cell and change a woman's life. Despite the number of known risk factors for breast cancer, however, most women with the disease have no risk factors other than their gender or their age. Joan, who developed breast cancer in her forties, says with humor, "I was so surprised that I had breast cancer because there is no history of it in my family. My first thought was, 'Oh, no! My sisters are gonna kill me!'"[12]

CHAPTER TWO

Symptoms and Diagnosis

In 1982 an organization called the Susan G. Komen Breast Cancer Foundation was established in memory of Susan G. Komen, who died of breast cancer in 1980, at the age of thirty-six. Since its inception, it has invested more than $1 billion into breast cancer research, education, and support for breast cancer patients and their families. Largely because of efforts such as this, a great deal has been learned about breast cancer and its treatment, and women are much more aware of the need for early diagnosis of this disease.

Today, most breast cancers are discovered at a much earlier stage than they were thirty years ago, and usually before any symptoms appear. However, many cases still go undiagnosed until symptoms appear and the woman seeks medical attention. The first signs of breast cancer usually involve a noticeable change in the appearance or feel of the breast or nipple.

Early Signs

The most common, early sign of breast cancer is a thickening or lump felt in or around the breast or the axilla. A lump that is painless and feels hard, with uneven edges, is more likely to be cancer; however, it may also be breast cancer when a mass feels soft and rounded and possibly painful. An important exception to this is inflammatory breast cancer, which does

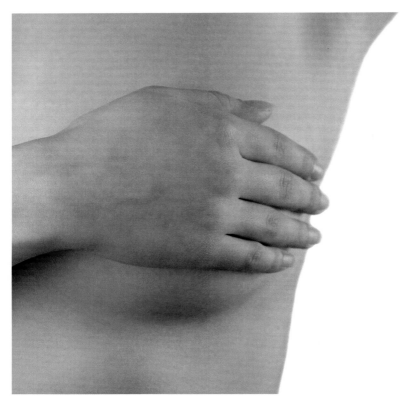

It is important for women to perform monthly breast self-examinations to look for changes in the appearance or feel of the breast or nipple. These changes are usually the most common early warning sign that breast cancer may be present.

not form lumps but grows in a sheet-like pattern and invades the skin of the breast.

Another early sign is a change in the size or shape of the breast. James, a British man who developed breast cancer in his late forties, discovered his cancer this way. "I discovered my lump by accident," he says. "I was in the gym changing room and glanced across at a mirror. I noticed that my chest looked a little unbalanced, that the right side appeared bigger. When I had a closer look, there was a lump about the size of a fifty pence piece [slightly larger than a quarter] to the left of my right nipple. It felt hard to the touch. Of course, it never occurred to me that I might have breast cancer. How wrong I was."[13]

Changes in the look or feel of the nipple are also important signs of possible breast cancer. There may be a discharge of blood or fluid from the nipple. The fluid may be clear, or it may be whitish or yellowish in color. The nipple may also become inverted, or turned inward, looking as if it has sunken into the breast. Patsy, who was diagnosed with Stage I breast cancer, discovered her cancer because of these symptoms. "I just happened to be at home and saw a person on TV say, 'You don't have to have a lump to have breast cancer,'" she says. "The lady said any discharge from the nipple, inverted nipple, or itching from the nipple area could mean that you have cancer. I was in shock. I had every one of them."[14]

Many of these symptoms can be caused by other, noncancerous conditions such as infections or hormonal changes, but any changes in the breast should always be brought to the attention of a physician.

Testing for Breast Cancer

Tests related to breast cancer fall into three main categories—screening, diagnostic, and monitoring. Screening tests are given to healthy people who do not suspect that they have cancer. "A screening test tries to find a disease before there are any symptoms," says Dr. Susan G. Orel, Professor of Radiology at the Hospital of the University of Pennsylvania. "With breast cancer, there's a misconception that if you feel fine, don't have a lump, and have no family history of breast cancer, you're okay. The truth is that three quarters of the women in whom we find breast cancer have no risk factors. So screening is important for everyone."[15]

Diagnostic tests are given to women who have either developed symptoms of breast cancer, or whose screening test has turned up an area of suspicion. These tests either rule out breast cancer, or they confirm breast cancer and help doctors decide on a course of treatment. Monitoring tests are done during and after breast cancer treatment. They help doctors evaluate the effectiveness of treatment and check for recurrences and metastasis.

Mammograms

By far, the most common screening test for breast cancer is the mammogram. A mammogram is an X-ray of the breast that uses a low dose of radiation to create an image of the inside of the breast. Mammograms can detect several abnormalities. For example, calcifications—tiny grain-like pieces of calcium in the breast tissue—can sometimes be a sign of an early breast cancer before a lump can be felt. Mammograms can also detect cysts—fluid-filled masses which are almost never cancer. They can also detect fibroadenomas, which are very common benign breast masses. A woman named Marcia tells why she was

A woman receiving a digital mammogram as a screening for breast cancer. Digital mammograms are used in place of regular mammograms when a woman has dense breasts and a regular mammogram may not be able to detect breast cancer because of the dense tissue.

glad she had a mammogram, "I wasn't looking for surprises," she says. "I just wanted to keep watch over my health with a routine mammogram. Something [in the test results] worried somebody, because I had to have more pictures. Then a biopsy. I thought it would be just a needle stick—but it was a real operation. I can't complain. It was benign. I'm okay."[16]

Mammograms have been in use since the mid-1960s. "Mammography plays a critical part in diagnosing breast cancer," says Dr. Orel. "In the past, we'd often find that a woman had breast cancer when she came in with a lump. Today, the cancers radiologists find on mammography are usually detected early, before they can be felt by the patient, are smaller than cancers felt by patients, and have much lower levels of lymph node involvement."[17] Mammograms have been shown to decrease the risk of dying from breast cancer by as much as 35 percent in women over fifty. Most cancer experts recommend that women over forty (younger if the woman is at high risk) get a screening mammogram once a year.

During mammography, a highly trained technician positions the breast between two clear plates, which are connected to a specialized camera. The plates are brought together, which gently compresses the breast to spread out and reduce the thickness of the tissue so that a more accurate image is obtained. Images are taken in two directions—from top to bottom and from side to side—and printed out onto X-ray film. The compression can be somewhat uncomfortable, but it only takes a few seconds to take the images, and the entire procedure takes about twenty minutes.

Women who have very dense breast tissue and are worried that a regular mammogram may miss an early cancer may opt to have a digital mammogram. A digital mammogram also uses X-rays, but the images are recorded directly into a computer rather than onto film. The images can be enlarged and examined more closely, especially if there is an area of suspicion. They can also be sent to other computers for review by additional doctors. One disadvantage is that the equipment is much

Computer-Aided Detection and Diagnosis (CAD)

Computer-aided detection and diagnosis, or CAD, is a method of using specialized computer software to focus very closely on a particular area of concern found on a digital mammogram. If the mammogram is on film, it is fed into a machine that can convert it to a digital image. The CAD software can highlight areas of concern with markers right on the viewing screen.

CAD has been available since 1998, but research into its effectiveness at making more accurate readings of mammograms has not shown a clear advantage. There is no clear evidence yet that CAD provides more accurate readings than having a second radiologist read the mammogram. A possible disadvantage is that CAD can render a reading that interprets normal changes as possible cancers—a "false positive" reading—that can lead to more tests and even surgery where no cancer exists. A 2007 study of more than 220,000 women showed that those who got their mammograms done at facilities that had CAD technology were more likely to have their mammograms read as abnormal, and then had to have a biopsy to rule out cancer. Despite these issues, as CAD technology improves, it is likely that it will become a more common diagnostic tool for use with mammograms.

more expensive, so the cost may be higher, and the equipment is not as widely available as regular film mammography.

Breast Exams

Even though mammograms are very accurate and valuable tools for detecting early breast cancers, as many as 20 percent of breast cancers may not show up on a mammogram, especially if the breast tissue is very dense. Another screening test which is also valuable for catching breast cancer early is the breast exam, done either by a doctor or by the woman herself.

A clinical breast exam is done by a doctor in the office during the woman's routine, yearly physical examination. The doctor checks for any changes in the size or shape of the breasts and for changes in the skin or the nipple. The doctor then uses a diagnostic technique called palpation to check for lumps in the breast. Using small, circular motions around the entire surface of the breast, the doctor gently presses to make sure there are no masses in the breast tissue or fluid discharge from the nipples. The doctor will also palpate the axilla and the area under the collarbone to check for enlarged lymph nodes.

Breast self-exam (BSE) is very similar to the clinical exam, except that it is done at home by the woman. During BSE, the woman looks in the mirror to check for the same signs the doctor does during a clinical breast exam. She then lies down and checks her breasts and armpits for lumps, using the fingertips to palpate the entire surface. Many women have found their own breast cancers before they were seen on a mammogram. Most doctors recommend that women do BSE at least once a month, in addition to having a yearly, clinical exam.

Diagnostic Tests

Diagnostic tests for breast cancer are done when cancer is suspected after a screening test, and the diagnosis needs to be confirmed. They are also done as follow-up testing for women who have already been treated for breast cancer. Other diagnostic tests are done on the tissue itself to determine if it is breast cancer and, if it is, to determine the particular type of breast cancer involved.

Mammograms can be used for diagnostic, as well as screening, purposes. Dr. Cecilia Brennecke,, a breast imaging specialist at Johns Hopkins University in Baltimore, explains the difference:

A routine or screening mammogram consists of four views—two views of each breast. The technologist takes the pictures, checks them for quality, and then you leave. With a diagnostic mammogram, you start with four standard views, and then supplement them with additional views, a physical exam, and ultrasound and MRI as needed. So a diagnostic mammogram is for women who are having a problem such as a lump or unusual nipple discharge or pain. A diagnostic mammogram is generally read by the radiologist right after it has been done. Ideally the woman does not leave the radiology facility until she has an answer about what is causing her breast problem. Usually the outcome is that everything is fine, but there is a higher incidence of finding cancer in that situation than in a screening situation.[18]

Ultrasound

Ultrasound is a very commonly used diagnostic tool, useful in many areas of medicine. It uses very high-frequency sound waves, too high to be detected by the human ear. The ultra-

A patient may receive an ultrasound on the breast to determine if a mass found in the breast is actually a tumor or cyst.

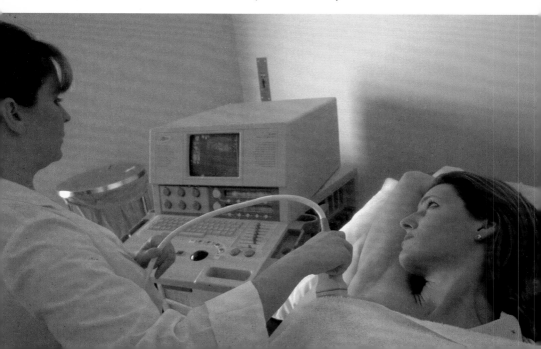

sound technician moves a special probe over the area of the breast to be examined. The probe sends the sound waves into the breast. The sound waves bounce back off the tissue at different rates, depending on the density of the tissue with which they come in contact. The ultrasound machine converts the reflected sound waves into an image on a screen. The best use of a breast ultrasound is to determine if a mass in the breast is solid or if it is a fluid-filled cyst. A solid tumor will appear whitish on the screen, but a cyst will appear black because the sound waves travel right through fluid rather than reflect off of it.

Magnetic Resonance Imaging (MRI)

An MRI is another method of creating images of the inside of the breast or other parts of the body. There is no radiation with an MRI, as there is with a mammogram. It uses radio waves and magnets to produce cross-sectional images. MRIs are useful in breast cancer diagnosis in several ways. They can be used to screen women who have very dense breast tissue or are already known to be at high-risk for breast cancer, for helping to learn more about a suspicious area seen on a mammogram or ultrasound, for evaluating lymph nodes that contain breast cancer cells when there is no apparent mass in the breast, or as a monitoring test for women who have already been treated for breast cancer and need to be checked for recurrences or metastases.

Biopsies

Imaging tests such as mammograms, ultrasounds, and MRIs, along with physical breast exams, may raise the suspicion of breast cancer, but they cannot absolutely confirm the diagnosis. The only way to do this is to take a biopsy—a sample of the tissue in the area of concern—and examine it under a microscope for the presence of cancer cells.

There are several ways to get a biopsy. The method used is determined by the size of the breast or the abnormal area, where in the breast it is located, and the preferences of the

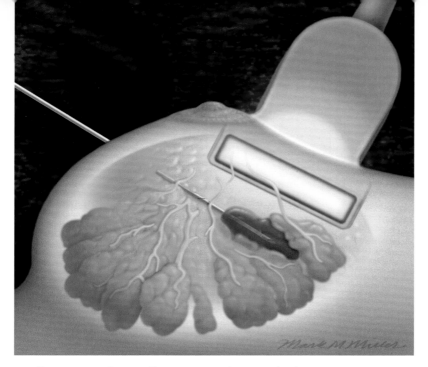

An illustration of a needle aspiration biopsy, the least invasive method in which to obtain a sample of cells. In this case the ultrasound is being used to help position the needle in the correct location of the area of concern.

doctor and the patient. Needle aspiration is the least invasive method. After numbing the skin with a local anesthetic, the doctor inserts a small needle that is attached to a syringe, into the breast to collect and remove a sample of cells. If the area is difficult to palpate, the doctor may use ultrasound or mammography to help position the needle in the correct location. The procedure only takes a few minutes.

Similar to needle aspiration, is a core biopsy. This procedure uses a slightly larger needle. As the needle is inserted, breast tissue cells fill the hollow interior of the needle. The needle is removed and the sample is taken out of the needle for examination. In both procedures, several samples are taken to help ensure an accurate result.

Surgical Biopsy

Needle biopsies and core biopsies are quick, relatively painless, and leave no scar, but because they take a very small sample of tissue, there is a risk that the cancer might be missed and lead to a false negative result. The doctor may recommend a surgical biopsy instead. Surgical biopsies are done in a hospital or outpatient surgery center, usually under local anesthesia, with some sedative medication given intravenously (through an IV). If the area is deep in the breast, or if the patient prefers, she can be given a general anesthetic and sleep through the procedure. In a surgical biopsy, an incision is made in the skin and the entire area of suspicion is removed, along with a small rim of tissue around it, called a margin. The tissue is then sent to the lab for microscopic examination by a pathologist, a physician who specializes in diagnosing tissue cell abnormalities.

If the suspicious area is difficult to feel, the patient may go to the mammography center before the surgery and have a tiny wire inserted into the area, guided by mammography. This is called needle localization. Small barbs at the end of the wire hold the wire in place at the suspicious area. The surgeon uses the end of the wire as a guide to help make sure he removes tissue from the correct area. The wire is left in the tissue sample, which is sent back to the mammography center. There, the tissue itself is X-rayed to make sure that the area of concern is included in the removed tissue.

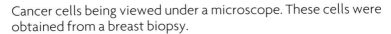

Cancer cells being viewed under a microscope. These cells were obtained from a breast biopsy.

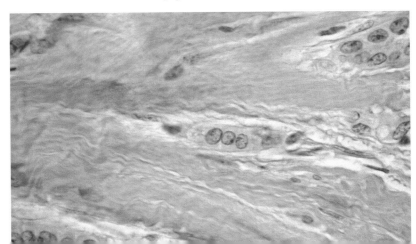

Examining the Biopsy

In the lab, the pathologist examines and tests the tissue and writes a report of his findings. First, he does a gross examination in which he describes the general appearance of the specimen—its size, weight, color, and texture, and whether any palpable masses are present in it. Then he does a microscopic exam. The tissue is bathed in a fixative solution, usually formaldehyde, to preserve it in the condition it was at the time of removal. After fixation, the tissue is put into a machine that removes all the water from it. It is then embedded in hot wax to make a tissue block. When the tissue block hardens, very thin slices are shaved from it and put under a microscope for examination of the cells.

In his report, the pathologist will describe the grade of the cancer—how abnormal the cells are and how aggressive the cancer is likely to be. He will also determine the stage of the cancer—whether or not it has spread outside of the ducts or lobules and into the breast tissue around it. Then, using special stains, he will examine the tissue for the presence of certain kinds of protein—hormone receptors and genetic markers—which can indicate what type of cancer is involved and what type of treatment is likely to work best.

Hormone Receptors

If the biopsy is positive for cancer, one of the most important things that it will be tested for is the presence of estrogen receptors or progesterone receptors in the cancer cells. Estrogen and progesterone are female hormones that have very important functions in female sexual development and pregnancy. Estrogen also has an important role in healthy bone and heart function. The breasts, uterus, heart, and bones are all estrogen and progesterone target tissues. They have no effect on any tissues other than their target tissues.

Hormone receptors are specialized protein molecules on the surface of the cells of target organs, such as the breast, that allow the target organ to respond to the "messages" that the hormone brings. Of the two hormones, estrogen has the most impact on the development of breast cancer. A group of researchers from Cornell University in New York explain how estrogen receptors work: "Estrogen has a shape that allows it to fit into an estrogen receptor in the same way a key fits into a lock. The estrogen and the estrogen receptor bind to form a unit that enters the nucleus of the cell. The estrogen-receptor unit binds to specific sites on the cell's DNA, and this begins a series of events that turns on estrogen-responsive genes. These specialized genes instruct the cell to make proteins that carry out important activities. Some of these signaling proteins can tell the cell to divide."[19] Since estrogen stimulates cell division in its target organs, any mutation in the cell's DNA can become permanent as the cells divide and pass on the mutation to new cells. This is how estrogen helps some breast cancers to grow.

About 30 to 60 percent of breast cancers have estrogen or progesterone receptors on their cells and rely on the presence of estrogen to keep growing. These tumors are said to be ER-positive or PR-positive. A tumor that is low in hormone receptors is called ER-negative or PR-negative. If a tumor's cells are ER-positive, doctors can prescribe a course of hormonal treatment that includes drugs called anti-estrogens, which interfere with the effect of estrogen on the cancer cells. The more receptors that are present, the more likely the tumor is to respond well to anti-estrogen hormone therapy.

HER-2 Testing

About 25 percent of all breast cancers are referred to as HER-2 positive. HER-2 stands for human epidermal growth factor receptor 2. HER-2 is a gene that is present in normal breast cells. The gene is responsible for the production of HER-2 protein, which regulates cell growth and reproduction.

A HER-2 positive cancer cell has an abnormally high number of copies of the HER-2 gene. This causes too much HER-2 protein to be on the surface of the cell. The cells then grow and divide abnormally fast. The HER-2 status of a breast cancer is very important to know because HER-2 positive breast cancer is particularly aggressive, and it may be more likely to recur in

Triple Negative Breast Cancers

Estrogen receptor-positive, progesterone receptor-positive, or both account for 30 to 60 percent of breast cancers. About 25 percent are HER-2 positive cancers. Having these three tumor markers present in the cancer cell makes them more susceptible to treatment methods such as anti-estrogen hormone therapy.

Approximately 15 percent of breast cancers do not have any of the three markers. They are known as "triple-negative" cancers. Triple negative cancers tend to be rather aggressive, do not respond well to treatment, and have a worse prognosis—a shorter survival time—no matter what stage they are in at the time of diagnosis. Research done in 2007 and 2009 showed that triple-negative cancers are three times more common in African American women than in Caucasian or Hispanic women. This helps to explain the fact that, although African American women get breast cancer less often, when they do get it, it tends to be more advanced when it is diagnosed, has a worse prognosis, and has a higher chance of recurring. This research points out the importance for women of all racial backgrounds to be very vigilant regarding their breast health.

the future. One reason why HER-2 positive breast cancers are so aggressive is because they are often associated with a protein called vascular endothelial growth factor (VEGF). VEGF stimulates angiogenesis—the growth of small blood vessels in the tumor that provides it with nutrients and oxygen and supports its growth. Another reason they are dangerous tumors is that they are usually ER-negative, so they do not respond well to hormone therapy.

Monitoring Tests

Monitoring tests are tests that are done after diagnosis and before, during, and after treatment. These tests help to estab-

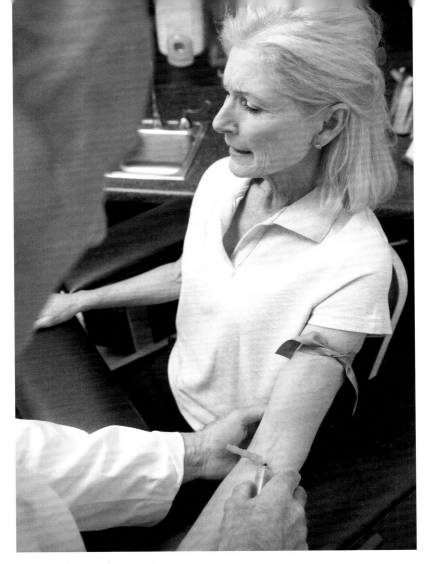

Among the first type of monitoring tests done on a breast cancer patient are blood tests. These tests help establish the patient's overall health before, during, and after treatment.

lish the overall health of the patient before starting treatment. They also assist doctors evaluate the effectiveness of the treatment, and allow the doctors to monitor the patient's health and strength during treatment. In addition, they are used to check for recurrence of the breast cancer and for metastasis to other parts of the body.

Among the first tests done are blood tests. A complete blood count, or CBC, shows the amounts of various kinds of blood cells present, such as white and red blood cells and platelets. White cells are part of the immune system and help fight off infections. Red cells are responsible for carrying oxygen to all the other cells in the body. Platelets have an important job in blood clotting. Cancer and its treatments can decrease the amounts of these important cells, so the cells are watched very closely. Another blood test frequently done during cancer treatment is blood chemistry. Blood chemistries give an indication of how well organs such as the liver, kidneys, and pancreas are functioning, so that any harmful effects of treatment on these organs can be managed. They also indicate if the patient is well-nourished enough.

Imaging Tests

Several different imaging studies are done for breast cancer patients to monitor the effectiveness of treatment and to watch for recurrence and metastasis. The patient is likely to get a chest X-ray to see if the cancer has spread to the lungs and to make sure the heart and lungs are healthy enough for anesthesia before surgery and for the stresses of cancer treatment.

Several different types of scans, including more MRIs, may be given. A CT (computerized tomography) scan is an imaging technique using X-rays that gives a detailed picture of the inside of the body in cross-sectional views. During a CT scan, the patient lies on a narrow table that moves slowly through a donut-shaped machine that takes X-rays from several different angles. A computer puts the images together to give a series of pictures. CT scans may be used to evaluate large cancers that may have spread to the chest wall, or they may show metastases in other organs.

A PET (positron emission tomography) scan is another kind of scan that can detect areas of cancer. A PET scan actually gives a picture of the body's cells at work. Previous to the scan, the patient is given a sugar solution with a small amount of radioactive material added, called a tracer. Cancer cells tend to take up, or absorb, the radioactive sugar faster than noncancerous cells. The areas of high uptake show up on a computer screen and indicate where doctors need to look for possible cancer cells. PET scans help identify cancer that has spread to lymph nodes or other parts of the body, and they help to assess the effectiveness of treatment.

A third type of scan is a bone scan, which shows whether breast cancer has spread to the bones. A bone scan may be done as soon as the diagnosis is made, to establish a baseline image for comparison at a later time, or to check for metastasis if the patient develops persistent pain in her bones and joints. During a bone scan, a radioactive tracer is injected into the bloodstream. The body is then scanned using a special type of camera. Areas of increased bone cell activity take up the material faster than areas of lower activity. These areas will show up as dark areas on the scan. Bone scans can also show other changes that are not cancer, such as arthritis. If the scan shows "hot spots" in the spine or joints, more testing may be needed to determine if they are caused by cancer or arthritis.

Thanks to improved methods of screening, many breast cancers are detected very early. Testing for hormone receptors and genetic markers further refine the diagnosis, which allows for more personalized treatment options for each patient and improves the chances for a positive outcome.

CHAPTER THREE

Treatment of Breast Cancer

One of the reasons that cancer is so feared is that it can be very difficult to treat or cure. In their book, *Breast Cancer: The Facts You Need to Know About Diagnosis, Treatment, and Beyond,* Pat Kelly and Mark Levine write, "Cancer is not something that invades our body from the outside like a virus or a bacteria; cancer is not like an injury or a trauma. Cancer is a disease of the self: the body's own cells change and grow out of control. That is why it is so hard to stop cancer cells from growing . . ."[20] Complicating the issue is the fact that even within the same cancerous tumor, there may be different types of cancer cells. Even though all the cells in a tumor begin with a breast tissue cell, as a cancer grows, the cells that make it up change, and new types of cancer cells are created within the same tumor mass. Each type has its own particular DNA "fingerprint." A treatment method that works on one type of cell, may not work on another. For this reason, a combination of treatment methods are used in a carefully planned sequence, in order to get rid of as many different types of cancer cells as possible.

A diagnosis of breast cancer was once little better than a death sentence, but that is no longer the case. "In recent years," according to the Web site Breastcancer.org, "there's been an explosion of life-saving treatment advances against breast cancer, bringing new hope and excitement. Instead of only one or two options, today there's an overwhelming menu of treatment choices that fight the complex mix of cells in each individual cancer. The decisions—surgery, then perhaps radiation, hormonal (anti-estrogen) therapy, and/or chemotherapy—can feel overwhelming."[21]

Planning Treatment

Once the initial confusion and flurry of information after diagnosis has settled, it is time for the patient and her physicians to work very closely together to decide on the most appropriate treatment options for her particular case. "When you're in the midst of the diagnosis and staging process, and the tumor information is coming back in bits and pieces, at many different times, it is an extremely stressful time in your life," says Dr. Marisa Weiss, breast cancer expert and founder of the Web site Breastcancer.org. "But you will feel SO much better once you know what you're dealing with, when your treatment plan has been worked out, and you start your treatment. Only then does much of that dreadful uncertainty lift, and you finally feel that you are doing something to get rid of the problem."[22]

After receiving her diagnosis it is important for a breast cancer patient to work closely with her physicians in planning the best treatment options for her particular case.

Treatment of Breast Cancer

The goal of breast cancer treatment is either to get rid of the cancer completely and achieve a total cure, or at least to slow its growth, keep it from spreading, and help the person live for as long as possible. There are many options for treating breast cancer, and the methods chosen will depend on the specific type of cancer involved, the personal wishes of the patient, and the recommendation of the doctor. Treatment methods include different kinds of surgeries, chemotherapy, hormone therapies, and radiation therapy.

Surgery for Breast Cancer

Surgery is often the first step in breast cancer treatment, depending on the nature of the cancer, its stage, and the personal needs of the patient. Many breast cancer patients have the option of having the entire breast removed, called a mastectomy, or they might choose breast-sparing surgery, called a lumpectomy, followed by radiation therapy and possibly chemotherapy. With either option, lymph nodes may or may not be removed as well.

Lumpectomy

A lumpectomy is a surgical procedure in which only the cancerous area is removed, along with a portion of normal tissue around it, called the tumor margin. It is similar to a surgical biopsy, except that it is for treatment rather than for diagnosis, so more tissue is removed to increase the likeliness of removing all of the cancerous cells in the tissue. Like biopsies, lumpectomies may be done under local anesthesia (which causes a temporary loss of feeling in a particular area of the body, while maintaining consciousness) or general anesthesia (which causes a temporary loss of consciousness). A lumpectomy takes about half an hour to complete.

Depending on the size of the tumor, the amount of tissue removed may be fairly small, or it may be as much as a quarter of the breast. If the suspicious area is small and difficult to feel, the patient may have needle localization first, just as it might be done before a biopsy, to help the surgeon locate the right area and to assure that he takes enough of a margin around the area. The tissue removed is sent to the laboratory for gross and microscopic examinations. It is examined for the presence of cancer cells in the margins. If there are no cancer cells in the margins around the mass, they are said to be clear. If one or more of the margins are not clear, and cancer cells are found there, another surgery will need to be performed so that the surgeon can remove more tissue from that area.

When the procedure is done and the patient awakens from the anesthesia, she can go home. The doctor will prescribe pain medication for her to take at home if she needs it. A lumpectomy is often followed by a course of radiation therapy. Chemotherapy may also be used as a follow-up treatment. These additional treatments are administered in an effort to achieve complete removal of all cancer cells in, and around, the affected area.

Mastectomy

A mastectomy is the removal of the entire breast. This procedure is recommended if the tumor is more than 5 centimeters in size, the breast is very small, clear tumor margins cannot be obtained, or the patient wants there to be no chance of the cancer coming back in the same breast. Depending on the type and stage of the cancer, mastectomy may also be recommended for tumors smaller than 5 centimeters. It is always done under general anesthesia and usually involves a hospital stay of two to three days. There are several different types of mastectomies, depending on how much tissue is actually removed.

A simple, or total, mastectomy involves removal of all of the breast tissue, but no lymph nodes are removed from the axilla. A simple mastectomy is an option for women who have the noninvasive DCIS, which is unlikely to spread. Women who are already scheduled for breast cancer surgery may opt to have a simple mastectomy on the other side as well, to avoid any chance of the cancer occurring in the other breast. This is

Minimally Invasive Lumpectomy

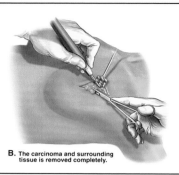

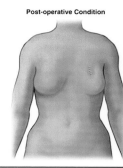

Post-operative Condition

A. The area of malignancy is identified and a small incision is made to access the diseased tissue.

B. The carcinoma and surrounding tissue is removed completely.

Modified Radical Mastectomy

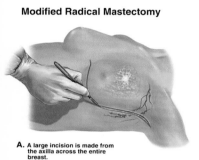

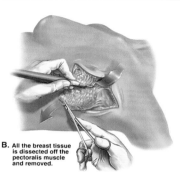

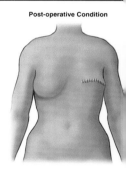

Post-operative Condition

A. A large incision is made from the axilla across the entire breast.

B. All the breast tissue is dissected off the pectoralis muscle and removed.

Two illustrations showing the difference between a lumpectomy and a mastectomy. In a lumpectomy just the cancerous tumor and surrounding tissue is removed, while in a mastectomy the entire breast is removed.

called a prophylactic mastectomy, because it prevents cancer from occurring in the healthy breast.

A modified radical mastectomy involves removal of all of the breast tissue, as well as many of the lymph nodes in the armpit. A woman will need a modified radical mastectomy if it has already been determined that the cancer has spread to the nodes. The nodes are removed so that they can be examined for the presence of cancer cells—a procedure called an axillary node dissection. Determining the number of nodes that are positive for cancer helps in staging the breast cancer and in making decisions about further treatment methods. At the end of the procedure, just before the incision is closed, the surgeon will insert two to three drains—long narrow tubes which are attached to small collection bulbs that apply gentle suction to the inside of the incision. Blood and cell fluids often build up inside a surgical incision and can cause pain, infection, and delayed healing. The drain helps to draw the fluids out of the incision into the bulb and keep them from collecting inside the incision.

Another type of mastectomy is a skin-sparing mastectomy. In this mastectomy, a much smaller incision is made. Only the nipple, the areola, and the skin over the original biopsy site are removed, and the breast tissue is removed through this smaller incision. This is an option for women who want to have their breast reconstructed by a plastic surgeon immediately after the breast is removed, during the same operation. It is not an option if the tumor is very close to the skin, because there is too much of a chance that tumor cells will be left behind.

Sentinel Node Biopsy

During either a lumpectomy or a mastectomy, the patient may have an additional procedure called a sentinel node biopsy. The word "sentinel" means "to watch for" or "stand guard over." The idea behind a sentinel node biopsy is that, since cancer spreads outside the breast through the nodes, if the doctor can identify the first node that it would have spread to—the sentinel node—he can determine whether or not the cancer has spread.

When a woman who is scheduled for a sentinel node biopsy arrives at the hospital, she goes to the Nuclear Medicine Department, where procedures using radioactive substances are done. The area of the cancer is injected with a substance called a radioactive tracer. The tracer gives off very small amounts of radiation. After the injection, the woman goes on to the operating room, where the surgeon injects a blue dye into the same area. In the same way that cancer cells spread into the lymph nodes, the radioactive tracer and the blue dye are taken up by the nodes.

Complementary Breast Cancer Treatments

Many people feel that, while doctors do a great job of treating disease, they sometimes may overlook or forget other needs of the patient—spiritual, mental, and emotional needs. Many patients and health care providers believe that the mind and the body are very closely connected, and that successful treatment of disease requires attention to both. Treatment therapies that address these needs are called complementary, or holistic, medicine. They are seen as more gentle and natural than traditional methods involving surgeries, radiation, and drugs. They are used as a complement to standard treatment—along with, not instead of, traditional methods.

There are hundreds of kinds of complementary methods. A few examples of complementary medicine therapies include yoga, meditation and relaxation techniques, herbal supplements, hyp-

Nancy had a sentinel node biopsy along with her mastectomy after she was diagnosed in 2008. In an on-line journal, she describes her experience: "About 7:45 am the radiology department came to get me to have the radioactive tracer injected for the sentinel node procedure. It only took about one minute, but it certainly did sting a lot. Doctor said it would be like a bee sting which it was ... a really big bee with attitude. Back to pre-op after that to just wait for my 11 am surgery time slot."[23]

After anesthesia is given and the patient is prepared for surgery, the surgeon makes a small incision near the armpit on the side of the cancer. He looks for a node that has been stained blue from taking up the dye that he injected earlier. He also uses a machine called a navigator, which can detect emissions of radioactive particles given off by the tracer. The navigator makes a series of clicking sounds that indicate how concen-

nosis, massage, music therapy, and acupuncture. While complementary medicine has not been shown to actually treat breast cancer, it may, for many people, improve the quality of their lives while they are undergoing regular treatments. For example, yoga has been shown to reduce fatigue, ease anxiety and stress, and improve sleep. Acupuncture is known to help relieve hot flashes, fatigue, nausea, vomiting, and pain. Like regular therapies, complementary therapies work better for some people than others, but many people feel that anything that may improve life is well worth a try.

Complimentary treatments, such as yoga, may help breast cancer patients to reduce fatigue, ease anxiety and stress, and improve sleep while undergoing traditional cancer treatments.

trated the radioactivity is. If the surgeon finds a node that is stained blue and also creates a lot of clicks on the navigator, it is considered to be a sentinel node. One to five nodes may be identified as sentinel nodes. The nodes are removed, sent to the lab, and examined microscopically for cancer cells. After Nancy's surgery, the news was good. "Dr. Smith said all went well and that the sentinel node was 'clean' with no cancer cells present. Great news! The sentinel node biopsy and the mastectomy took about 90 minutes, I was in recovery for about an hour and then up to my room by about 3:00 pm."[24]

If the sentinel nodes have no cancer cells, there is a 95 percent chance that the cancer has not spread out of the breast, and no further nodes need to be taken for staging purposes. If the sentinel node is positive for cancer cells, however, it means that the cancer has already spread outside the breast. In this case, an axillary node dissection is necessary, even if the patient only had a lumpectomy.

Sentinel node biopsy is very valuable because it helps a woman avoid having to have an axillary node dissection. This is important because the procedure can cause problems after surgery, such as numbness, weakness, or stiffness in the arm on the operative side. Another potential complication of axillary node dissection is called lymphedema, which occurs in about 10 to 12 percent of cases. When so many nodes are removed from the axilla, it changes the way that lymph fluid normally moves through the arm and upper body. This can cause swelling and pain in the arm that can interfere with normal use of the arm.

Chemotherapy
After surgery, the first course of treatment is often chemotherapy, commonly referred to as just "chemo." Chemotherapy is

A cancer patient receiving chemotherapy treatment while watching television. Chemotherapy may be administered through IV, injection, or orally.

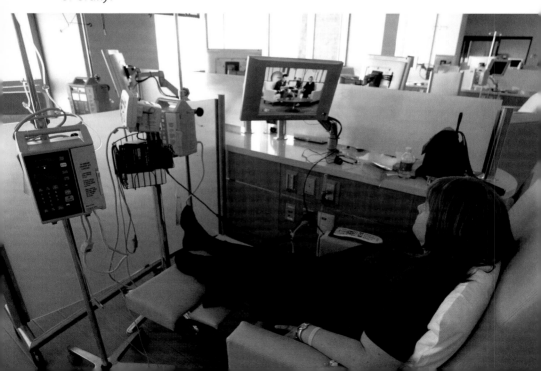

Classes of Chemotherapy Drugs

There are several categories of drugs that may be used during a course of chemo for breast cancer. Some of the drugs act in more than one way and may belong to more than one class. Alkylators are drugs that damage the DNA in the nucleus of the cancer cell and prevent it from duplicating. The most commonly used alkylator is cyclophosphamide (Cytoxan), which has been in use since the 1950s. Another class is the antimetabolites, which work by taking the place of the cancer cell's genes, so that it dies when it tries to divide and multiply. Common antimetabolites include Fluorocil, also called 5-FU, and methotrexate. Another class of drugs used in chemotherapy treatment is called antibiotics, but they are not the same kind of antibiotics as the ones given to treat infections. These antibiotics stop reproduction of the cancer cell's genes. A common drug in this class is Adriamycin. Antimitotic drugs, also called plant alkaloids, are often made from plants or other natural products. They also prevent genes from replicating themselves during cell division—a process called mitosis. Vincristine and vinblastin are antimitotic drugs.

the use of drugs to treat cancer. Its purpose is to destroy any cancer cells that may remain after surgery. It may also be given before surgery to help shrink the size of the tumor, so that the patient may have the option of having a lumpectomy instead of a mastectomy. It is a systemic treatment, meaning that the drugs travel through the bloodstream and can have their affect on cancer cells that may have already gone to other parts of the body. It also means that the drugs may affect healthy cells as well. Chemotherapy drugs can be given through an IV, by injection, or by mouth.

Chemo is given in cycles. Each visit to the doctor or hospital for a dose of chemo drugs is one cycle. A cycle consists of a treatment period, which may take a day or two, followed by a recovery period, during which the patient rests and recovers from the side effects of the drugs, which can be unpleasant and cause weakness and fatigue. A course of chemo includes anywhere from four to eight cycles, given every two to three weeks depending on the nature of the tumor and the kind of drugs chosen for the treatment.

Chemotherapy drugs work by interfering with the growth and multiplication of rapidly dividing cells such as cancer cells. The drugs also affect other areas of rapid cell growth, such as the blood, mouth, gastrointestinal tract, and hair. Many of the drugs' side effects are expressed in these areas, leading to symptoms such as fatigue, diarrhea, constipation, mouth sores, hair loss, and nausea with vomiting. Healthy cells, however, are able to recover from the effects of the drugs and resume normal function once the course of chemo is over.

Not all breast cancer patients are candidates for chemo. Each individual case is unique, and what may be advised for one patient may not be advised for another. Factors that doctors consider when deciding whether or not to prescribe chemo include the particular features of the cancer—its size and stage, hormone receptor status and HER-2 status, and whether or not lymph nodes are involved. Because of the side effects, the patient's overall health status is considered. It is usually given to younger women who have not yet gone through menopause because they tend to have more aggressive forms of cancer. Chemo is never given to women who have noninvasive in situ types of cancer because that type of cancer has almost no risk of spreading.

Hormone Therapy

Like chemotherapy, hormone therapy is also a systemic treatment for breast cancer, because it circulates throughout the body. It may be used after surgery to reduce the chances of the cancer coming back, or it may be used before surgery to decrease the size of the tumor. It can also be used to treat recurrent cancer or cancer that has spread. It may be given along with chemotherapy drugs, after a course of chemotherapy, or by themselves.

The drugs used in hormone therapy are derived from sex hormones that are naturally present in both the male and female human body. They are used to treat cancers that grow in response to these hormones. They work by preventing the cancer cells from using the hormones that they need in order to keep growing. They also work by preventing the body from making the hormones.

About two-thirds of all breast cancers respond to the female hormone estrogen. That is, they are ER-positive or PR-positive, or both. These tumors can be treated by giving drugs that block the effect of estrogen or reduce the amount of estrogen made in the body. Hormone therapy does not work for tumors that are negative for hormone receptors.

Several kinds of drugs are used in hormone therapy for breast cancer. Anti-estrogens, such as Tamoxifen, temporarily block estrogen receptors on the cancer cell, which prevents the estrogen from binding to the receptor. According to the American Cancer Society, taking Tamoxifen for five years after surgery decreases the chances of the cancer coming back by about 50 percent. Another drug called Faslodex, not only blocks the receptors, but also eliminates them altogether. It is used in older women whose cancer no longer responds to Tamoxifen. Aromatease inhibitors are another class of hormone therapy drugs. They work by blocking an enzyme called aromatase, which is responsible for estrogen production in the fat tissue of post-menopausal women. Other drugs work by shutting down production of estrogen in the ovaries of younger women, which essentially creates a drug-induced menopause (normally, the naturally occurring permanent end of menstruation that usually happens between age forty-five and fifty-five). Occasionally, male hormones may be given for advanced breast cancers that do not respond to other hormone therapy drugs.

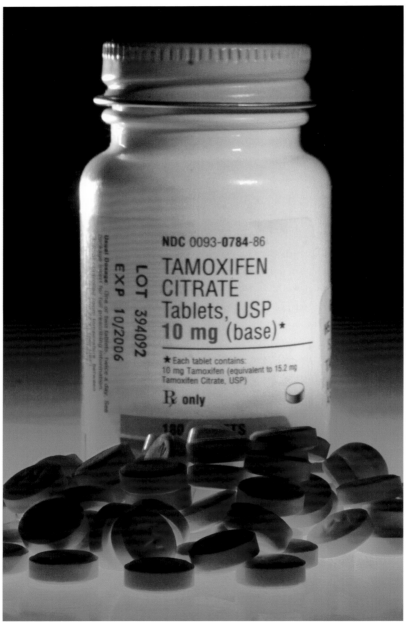

Tamoxifen is a type of hormone therapy known as an anti-estrogen. This type of therapy temporarily blocks estrogen receptors on the cancer cell and prevents the estrogen from binding to the receptor.

Radiation Therapy

After chemotherapy treatments are complete, the breast cancer patient may also have a course of radiation therapy. Radiation therapy, or radiotherapy, is a cancer treatment that uses high energy beams of radiation that destroy cancer cells. If chemotherapy is not going to be a part of the treatment plan, such as in noninvasive in situ cancers, radiation therapy may begin very soon after surgery.

Radiation damages cells by interfering with their DNA, thus interfering with their ability to grow and duplicate themselves. Radiation therapy is often a part of the treatment plan, because even with clear margins, there is never an absolute guarantee that every last cancer cell is removed. Remaining cancer cells can continue to grow and form a new tumor. Radiation therapy helps lower the risk that cancer will recur after surgery. Many research studies have demonstrated that women with Stage 0 through Stage III cancers who have a lumpectomy or a mastectomy followed by radiation therapy have a lower chance of the cancer coming back than women who do not have radiation, even if the cancer is very small. It can also be helpful for women with Stage IV cancer that has already spread.

Like chemo, radiation damages healthy cells as well as cancer cells, but healthy cells are more able to repair themselves after radiation treatment than cancer cells are. Dr. Marisa Weiss explains, "Cancer cell growth is unwieldy and uncontrolled—these cells just don't have their act together like normal cells do. When normal cells are damaged by radiation, they are like a big city with a fire and police department and trained emergency squads to come and 'put out the fire.' Damaged cancer cells are more like a disorganized mob with a bucket."[25]

Delivering Radiation Therapy

There are two main ways to deliver radiation therapy—externally, from outside the body, and internally, with implanted devices that deliver radiation from the inside. External beam radiation is the most common type of radiation therapy. It is usually started about a month after chemotherapy is com-

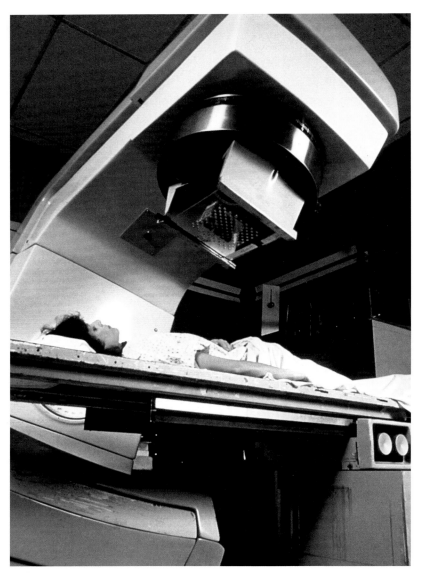

A breast cancer patient receiving external beam radiation, the most common form of radiation therapy.

pleted, or about three to six weeks after surgery if chemotherapy is not given. It is delivered using a machine called a linear accelerator, which aims the radiation beam right at the area where the cancer was. It is delivered to the whole breast (if only a lumpectomy was done) and may also include the area of the lymph nodes.

A course of external radiation treatments includes treatment sessions five days a week for five to seven weeks. Each treatment session lasts only a few minutes and is painless, but it can seem very strange for a person having their first treatment. Wendy describes her experience: "I start radiation on Monday. I've already been twice to get examined and 'marked' with little tattoo dots so they know where to line up the machine each time I go. It was a bizarre ritual in that they had me lay down on a table 'just so' with a huge round radiation thingy staring down on me and laser lights coming out of the walls and ceiling. I was waiting for a voice to say, 'Please remain seated until the ride has come to a complete stop.'"[26]

Internal radiation is also referred to as partial breast radiation, or breast brachytherapy. The term "brachy" means "short distance," and brachytherapy administers radiation to a more focused area of the breast by placing radioactive pellets directly into the breast, near the area of the cancer. It can be started immediately after surgery, or it can be given as a boost to a course of external beam radiation. Some recent research has suggested that brachytherapy may be just as effective as external beam radiation and carries less risk of damaging healthy tissue. Another advantage to brachytherapy is that the entire course of treatment lasts only five days instead of five to seven weeks. Women who benefit the most from brachytherapy include those who have early stage cancer, who have more advanced cancer that has not yet metastasized, or whose cancer has recurred in the chest wall and may not be treatable with more surgery.

There are two methods of delivering breast brachytherapy. Both of them involve minor surgery and require anesthesia. The first is called interstitial, or "tube and button," brachytherapy. In this procedure, a group of small tubes are placed through the breast in the area of the lumpectomy. The tubes are held in place by a "button" on one end of each tube. The other ends of the tubes are each attached to a device called an afterloader, which contains radioactive pellets and delivers a small dose of radiation directly to the area.

The other method of brachytherapy is called balloon catheter delivery. In this procedure, done at the time of a lumpectomy, a small catheter, or tube, is inserted into the cavity left by a lumpectomy. At the inside end of the catheter is a balloon, which is inflated with a saline solution inside the cavity. The outside end of the catheter is attached to an afterloader, which delivers the dose of radiation to the center of the balloon and exposes only the area immediately around the lumpectomy site to the radiation.

Treatment for breast cancer can be extremely complex, confusing, and stressful, but few women would make a decision not to do everything possible. Jeannette was twenty-nine when she was diagnosed with both DCIS and inflammatory breast cancer. She underwent a bilateral mastectomy with axillary node dissection, chemo, radiation, and hormone therapy. "Cancer is a crap-shoot," she says. "There are so many factors to treatment and every person's biology reacts to treatment very differently. It's scary at first, but it is a fight that you begin as soon as you are diagnosed and never intend to quit. It's a commitment, sometimes a financial one, that takes a new-found strength because you MUST be your own advocate. Research, a knowledge-base, support, friends, etc., is essential to getting the treatment that's right for you."[27]

CHAPTER FOUR

Living With Breast Cancer

A diagnosis of breast cancer can be a devastating thing to hear, for both the woman and her family. There is often an immediate reaction of fear—of death; of the rigors of treatment, surgery, and recovery; of the possibility of metastasis; for the welfare of the family; and of many others. "It was like my whole world was falling apart," says Rita, who was diagnosed in 2005. "I felt like I had been punched in the stomach. I went into my office and I stood there and I just started crying."[28] The diagnosis can be just as frightening for the woman's husband as it is for her. "I couldn't go fix it," says Jody, whose wife, Jessie, was diagnosed with "very aggressive" cancer in 2006. "All I could do was hold her and tell her we'd make it better. I would be the rock for her."[29]

The breast cancer patient must receive and process a great deal of information about the disease and its treatment. One of the first goals of the health care team is to reassure the woman that she has options, that her cancer can be treated, and there will be support for her and her family along the way. With the help of her doctors and her family, several very important decisions must be made very soon after diagnosis.

Decisions About Surgery

One of the first decisions to be made involves surgery. For patients who are able to choose between a lumpectomy and a

Women diagnosed with breast cancer should carefully research their options before making a decision regarding surgery.

mastectomy, the decision can be a complicated one. Research studies have shown that a lumpectomy with radiation is just as effective as a mastectomy in terms of long term survival from breast cancer, as long as the tumor is less than 4 centimeters in size and the tumor margins are clear. Each option has advantages and disadvantages.

The major advantage to a lumpectomy is that it preserves more of the natural size and shape of the breast. It usually does not require an overnight hospital stay, and recovery time is shorter and with less discomfort than with a mastectomy. One potential disadvantage is that as much as five to seven weeks of radiation therapy is required after a lumpectomy, to make sure any remaining cancer cells are eliminated. Also, depending on the type and stage of the cancer, there is some risk that the cancer will recur in the remaining breast tissue, or that a new cancer will develop there. If that happens, the patient will have to go back to surgery for a mastectomy.

A mastectomy has the advantage that it provides more peace of mind that the cancer will not come back on the same side, because all the breast tissue has been removed. Disadvantages are that it is more disfiguring than a lumpectomy, although reconstructive surgery is often possible. It is more extensive surgery, involving more anesthesia, a longer recovery time, and more discomfort. Radiation may or may not be needed, depending on the nature of the cancer.

Some women who are very concerned about breast cancer occurring in the other breast may opt to have the healthy breast removed as well. Having cancer in one breast increases the chance that it will show up on the other side as well, especially if there is a strong family history. Older women who may have a different emotional attitude about their breasts may decide to have both breasts removed, as might women for whom surgical reconstruction of the breasts is an option. One woman explains her decision, "My decision to have a double mastectomy was guided by my age, family history and attitudes about my breasts. I'd gained weight and had actually become uncomfortable with my breasts, and all my life I'd had a history of tenderness in my breasts. So I felt I wasn't going to miss them very much."[30]

Reconstruction

Another important decision to be made is whether or not to have surgical reconstruction of the breast. Approximately 75 percent of women who have mastectomies go on to have surgical reconstruction. Reconstructive breast surgery is done by a plastic surgeon. It does not actually create a new breast, of course, but it gives the woman the shape and feel of a new breast.

The simplest reconstruction method is the insertion of an artificial breast implant into a cavity created under the chest muscle. Breast implants come in many different shapes and sizes and are similar to a small water balloon. They consist of an outer shell made of silicone. The shell is inserted into the cavity. The plastic surgeon then fills it with either saline (a dilute salt water solution similar to natural tears) or silicone gel until it approximately matches the size of the remaining breast. The skin incision is then closed over the muscle. At a later time,

A silicone gel breast implant that will be used by a plastic surgeon in reconstructive surgery after a breast cancer patient has a mastectomy.

after the patient has healed completely and the rest of her treatment is complete, she may opt to have the nipple and areola also reconstructed, to make the new breast look more natural.

Tissue Flap Reconstructions

Tissue flap reconstructions are rather extensive surgeries that use skin, fat, and muscle from other areas of the patient's body to rebuild the breast. The most common methods are TRAM flaps and latissimus dorsi flaps.

TRAM stands for "transverse rectus abdominis muscle." This muscle is located in the lower abdomen. To perform a TRAM flap, the surgeon removes a portion of the muscle, along with its fat and skin, from the lower abdomen. Its blood vessels are left in place so that the flap keeps its blood supply, which is necessary for healing. A "tunnel" is created under the skin of the abdomen, and the tissue is passed through the tunnel and up into the space left by the mastectomy. The abdominal incision is closed and a new belly button is created. The tissue flap is shaped to closely match the other breast, and sewn in place.

A latissimus dorsi flap, or "lat flap," is similar to a TRAM except that the muscle used is the latissimus dorsi, located along the back side of the upper chest. This flap may be used instead of a TRAM if the woman is very obese and the rectus muscle is difficult to access, if she has already had a TRAM on the other side, or if she has multiple abdominal scars from other surgeries. As with a TRAM, the tissue flap is passed under the skin, around to the front, and sewn into place. An implant can be placed behind the flap, if necessary, to help match the other side.

Recovering from Surgery

Recovering from breast cancer surgery is, in some ways, not unlike recovering from other types of surgery. Once she is home from the hospital, the woman will need to rest, take pain medicines as needed, and watch the incision for signs of infection. She will need to rely on friends and family to help take care of daily needs at home.

If the woman has had an axillary node dissection along with the mastectomy, the doctor or nurse will teach the woman special exercises she can do to prevent stiffness and maintain mobility of her arm. These exercises must be done every day to keep the arm flexible and help prevent lymphedema—the swelling in the arm that can sometimes occur because of the removal of the lymph nodes in the axilla.

Another aspect of recovery from breast surgery is coping emotionally with the loss of the breast, especially if reconstructive surgery is not done. Many women, especially younger women, go through a period of grieving that has little to do with having cancer. Losing a breast can have serious implications for her self-esteem and confidence as a woman. She may no longer feel attractive to her partner or spouse. It is very important for the woman to talk about these feelings with those who

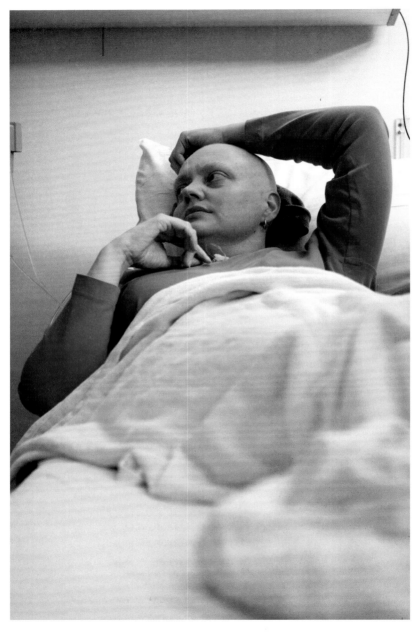

While recovering from breast cancer surgery, the patient will need lots of rest and may need to rely on friends and family for help around the house.

are close to her and to focus on what is positive in her life, so that she can still feel like a beautiful woman.

Side Effects of Treatment

After the surgery is done and healing is complete, the treatment plan may include chemotherapy, radiation, hormone therapy, or a combination of several treatment modalities. Although the treatments are designed to target cancer cells, they also affect healthy cells as well, so unpleasant side effects may occur. Side effects are undesired symptoms caused by the effects of treatment on other areas of the body. Most side effects are temporary and go away after treatment. Others may be chronic and last for a longer time.

Of the different treatment therapies, chemotherapy has the most side effects. "I think half the battle for me last week was just not knowing what to expect," writes Wendy, after her first chemo treatment. "The treatment itself on Wednesday was fine as was the next day (pretty much). But Friday and Saturday I felt like I was hit by a truck. I felt very flu-like . . . but different. I'm not sure I can fully explain. I never actually got sick but was just downright miserable—nausea, constant HUGE headache, dizzy, achy and I couldn't sleep very well because I had to go to the bathroom every hour and I also had the craziest dreams. I have weird dreams anyway . . . but these were different . . . almost like I was "plugged in."[31]

Chemotherapy damages cancer cells because it works on cells that divide rapidly, so other cells in the body that also divide rapidly, such as those in the blood, mouth, gastrointestinal tract, and hair, are also affected by it. It is almost impossible to predict which side effects a woman will have, because it depends on which drugs she is being given and on her body's particular response to the drugs. Some common, but temporary, side effects of chemotherapy include fatigue, nausea and vomiting, hair loss, mouth sores, menopausal symptoms such as hot flashes, numbness or tingling in the hands or feet, and memory problems. Other side effects that are more serious and may cause long term problems include blood changes, bone

Weight Lifting for Breast Cancer

For many years, doctors have counseled patients not to do any heavy lifting after breast cancer surgery, because it was thought that it would worsen lymphedema, the swelling in the arm that may accompany a mastectomy that includes removal of the lymph nodes in the armpit. Instead, they had been given special, nonweight-bearing exercises to do following surgery. A 2009 study headed by Dr. Kathryn Schmitz of the University of Pennsylvania may change that thinking. Dr. Schmitz found that, not only did weight lifting not worsen lymphedema, but it also had some benefits for the breast cancer patient. In her study, half of the participants were told not to do any extra exercise. The other half participated in ninety-minute weight classes twice a week for thirteen weeks. The classes included stretching and cardiovascular exercise as well as strength training. After the thirteen weeks, they continued the workouts on their own. After one year, only 14 percent of them had symptoms of lymphedema, compared to 29 percent of the women who did not lift weights. Those who exercised also had far fewer visits to doctors because of lymphedema symptoms, and they had greater strength and mobility in their arms. The study is now shifting focus to determine if weight lifting can help prevent lymphedema from becoming a side affect at all.

loss (osteoporosis), and damage to the heart. Fortunately, scientists have been able to develop very effective methods to minimize side effects and manage them when they do occur.

As many as 80 percent of patients experience some amount of chemotherapy-induced nausea and vomiting (CINV). It usually lasts for a just few hours, but can last for several days. It is important for the woman getting chemo to let her doctor know if she is experiencing CINV. Barbara Reville, a nurse practitioner and cancer treatment specialist in Philadelphia, Pennsylvania, says, "If you have problems with symptoms, they can be improved. You should call. I get very upset if someone says, 'I was throwing up,' but they never called. I hate that, because we could have helped them, if we had known."[32] The woman experiencing CINV can help control this side effect by eating several smaller, lighter meals, avoiding foods high in fat, and by staying upright for two to three hours after meals. Antinausea medications called antiemetics are very helpful for reducing or even preventing CINV.

Alopecia

Another common side effect which may occur after a few cycles of chemo is hair loss (alopecia). Alopecia can be a very difficult side effect to deal with, especially at first. Michele, a breast cancer survivor, says, "Some days I didn't want anyone to see me or even have my husband look at me."[33] Not all chemo

Some breast cancer patients who lose their hair due to chemo may decide to cover their heads with a hat, wig, or decorative scarf.

drugs cause alopecia, and some women may just have thinning of their hair instead of total hair loss. Other women may lose the hair on all parts of their body, as well as their head.

Hair almost always grows back after chemo is complete, but interestingly, straight hair may grow back curly or thin hair may grow back thicker. It may even be a different color. "When you are waiting for your hair to grow," says Michele, "you spend a lot of time looking in the mirror, just waiting for a sign that you're going back to normal."[34] Women can try to help minimize the amount of hair loss by using gentle shampoos, cutting the hair short, using a low setting on the blow dryer, and avoiding chemical products such as permanents or dyes. If she does lose all her hair, she can, if she chooses, help preserve her appearance and protect her scalp by wearing a hat, scarf, or wig.

Effects on the Blood

Some chemo drugs can significantly lower the amounts of several types of blood cells. Neutropenia is the term for a low count of white blood cells, which are part of the immune system. Neutropenia can make a person more susceptible to infections, which may require hospitalization, and can weaken her to the point where further cancer treatment may be delayed. Anemia is a low count of red blood cells, which carry oxygen to all the cells of the body. Anemia can cause or worsen fatigue and weakness. A lower than normal amount of platelets in the blood, which are needed for proper clotting, is called thrombocytopenia. Low platelets can cause bruising or prolonged bleeding if the woman gets a cut. Most of these problems can be treated with medications or, if necessary, a transfusion of blood or platelets.

Fertility and Chemotherapy

Pre-menopausal women receiving hormonal therapy to stop the action of estrogen may experience symptoms similar to menopause, such as irregular or absent menstrual periods, hot flashes, mood swings, and loss of bone strength. Younger woman on chemo may worry about how it will affect her fer-

About half of breast cancer patients under the age of thirty-
five regain their fertilty and are able to have children after their
treatment has been completed.

tility—her ability to have children in the future. The younger
the woman is, the more likely it is that her ovaries will resume
normal function after chemo is completed, and she will be
able to get pregnant. About half of the patients under the age
of thirty-five resume regular menstrual cycles, and are fertile,
after treatment. Certain drugs, especially those called alkylators (such as Cytoxan), and higher doses of other chemo drugs
are more likely to cause permanent menopause. Other drugs,
such as methotrexate, have little effect on fertility.

Another concern is the effect of chemo drugs on the unborn
child if the woman is pregnant or if she becomes pregnant during treatment. Chemo drugs can cause genetic damage to immature eggs while they are still in the ovaries. They may also cause
birth defects in the unborn child as it develops. Methotrexate,
for example, is not likely to hinder fertility but may increase
the risk for spinal cord defects in the unborn baby. Most doc-

tors encourage women to wait at least six months after chemo is completed before trying to get pregnant.

Side Effects of Radiation

The side effects of radiation are usually not as severe as those from chemotherapy, and not every woman will experience them. Like chemo side effects, they are usually temporary and should go away when treatment is done. Also, as with chemo, the woman getting radiation therapy should make sure her doctor knows about any side effects she may experience, so that they can decide on the best way to manage them.

The most common side effect is skin irritation, similar to a sunburn, caused by the radiation. The skin may become reddened, sensitive, dry, or flaky. It may even blister or peel. It may be worse in the armpit or under the breast, where there is more skin friction. It may also be worse in fair-skinned women or women with large breasts. Skin irritation can be helped by staying out of the sun, avoiding very hot or very cold water, wearing loose clothing, and using a soothing lotion. Radiation may cause some tenderness or swelling in the breast or chest wall around the treated area. It may also worsen fatigue for some women. In addition, it can also cause certain heart or lung problems, such as difficult breathing, coughing, rapid or irregular heartbeat, and swelling in the legs. Like chemo, it may also lower white blood cell counts.

Helping Children Cope

For many women, especially women with young children, a major concern after being diagnosed with breast cancer is how to help their children cope with the challenges of fighting the disease. Kathleen McCue, a child life specialist and author of the book, *Someone I Love is Sick*, says that being open and honest with children right away is very important, including using the word "cancer." "Children will probably hear the word somewhere," she says, "so if you don't use the word yourself, as the parent, and they hear it somewhere else, they're going to be afraid."[35] Monica, a breast cancer survivor and mother of three who had a double mastectomy, says, "We told [the children] that I had cancer, that it might make me feel sick, that certain things might happen, but we don't know. Children are very knowledgeable now, and if you give them enough information, they're not going to be as scared." Involving the whole family in treatment decisions is also very important. "We actually discussed what kind of operation we were going to have," says Monica, "because it's just not me, it's the whole family."[36]

Focusing on being there for her children can give a woman strength at those times when she is feeling bad due to side effects of treatment or when she begins to lose hope. Kathy, a breast cancer patient, says, "As I was getting better, I started thinking, hopefully, I'm going to be able to hang around until my kids are all in school. And that progressed me to thinking, maybe I'll be here when they all go off to college!"[37]

Getting Support and Help

There are many sources of support for breast cancer patients: community support groups; religious organizations; and networks of friends, family, and coworkers can help with daily needs such as meals, errands, housework, and childcare at those times when energy is low. Marilyn, a breast cancer

For some breast cancer patients it can be helpful to join a support group and talk about how other women have dealt with the disease and the challenges it has posed.

patient, says, "You have to open up and let other people help you. The way I was able to do it was to realize that it helps them to help you. So you're actually doing them a favor by letting them help you!"[38]

It can be very helpful for a breast cancer patient to be able to talk with other women who have gone through the same experiences and challenges and have met them successfully. Most communities provide contact information to groups of other women who have or have had breast cancer and can help in

Reach to Recovery

One of the oldest support organizations for women with breast cancer is Reach to Recovery. It was founded in 1952, by Terese Lasser of New York City. During her hospital stay for breast cancer, she felt totally alone with her questions and fears. She took it upon herself to get the answers to her questions, and decided that no woman should have to face breast cancer alone. She began to visit other women who were struggling with cancer, and found that having the support of another person with similar experiences was mutually beneficial. Over time, the network grew, and in 1969, Reach to Recovery joined with the American Cancer Society and became a nationwide organization.

Reach to Recovery provides highly trained volunteers who are breast cancer survivors themselves. The volunteers are available to anyone who has been newly diagnosed with breast cancer, is undergoing treatment, or has completed treatment and is dealing with side effects or metastasis. They provide emotional support and current information to patients through personal visits on the phone, at home, or anywhere the patient wants to meet. Today, with financial support from several large companies and foundations, Reach to Recovery is available to breast cancer patients and their families in almost every community in the United States.

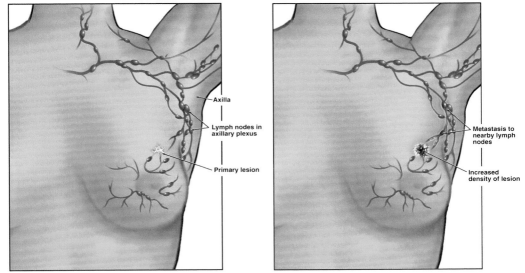

Anterior view of the left breast and axilla

Two illustrations showing a patient with breast cancer. The illustration on the left shows a noninvasive breast cancer, while the illustration on the right shows a regional recurrance due to the fact the cancer is again found in the lymph nodes of the axilla.

this way. For some women, spending some time talking with a therapist or clergy person can help relieve some of the emotional burden and help her learn effective ways to cope with anxiety or depression.

What if the Cancer Comes Back?

After surgery is done and treatment is completed, the fight is not over. There is always the fear that the cancer may come back, either in the same place or in another part of the body. Even a tiny number of cancer cells that escape surgery and treatment can grow and spread. Barbara, a breast cancer patient, says, "Living with the fear of breast cancer is having a whale move into your living room. One day, it just appears and is always in the way. Over time, the whale can get smaller, but it never quite goes away."[39] Psychiatric nurse Shari Baron runs support groups for women with breast cancer. "In my groups," she says, "we talk about 'BC' and 'AC'—Before Cancer and After Cancer. You can never go back to Before Cancer. You wonder: Will the cancer come back? The fear does lessen over time. But it's never gone completely."[40]

If breast cancer comes back in the same breast, or if it returns very close to the original place, it is called a local recurrence. Two thirds of breast cancers that come back are local recurrences. If cancer returns in a different part of the breast, or in the other breast, it is probably not a recurrence of the same cancer, but a new cancer altogether. It is even possible for a new cancer to appear after a mastectomy, in the few normal breast tissue cells that remain after surgery. Recurrences may be found by mammography, physical examination, or both. There may be extra tests such as an ultrasound or an imaging study, especially if the woman had reconstruction with an implant, to help determine if the new mass is really a recurrence of cancer or something harmless, such as scar tissue or an infection.

Breast cancer that comes back in the lymph nodes in the axilla, the neck, near the chest wall, or under the collarbone is called a regional recurrence. The woman may notice enlarged, round lumps in her arm pit or in her neck, or they may be seen on a follow-up mammogram. When this happens, it is likely that the cancer is back in the breast or chest wall, as well as the nodes. A surgical biopsy is done to check for cancer cells in the enlarged nodes.

Metastatic breast cancer is cancer that has traveled to some other part of the body, most commonly the bones, lungs, brain, or liver. It is usually found when the woman develops symptoms in the area to which it has spread. For example, symptoms of spread to the bones may include persistent back or joint pain, or numbness or tingling that may signal spread to the spine. In the brain, there may be headaches, blurred vision, confusion, or loss of balance. Spread to the lungs may cause a persistent cough, shortness of breath, or pain in the chest. Symptoms of spread to the liver may include abdominal pain, a yellowish color in the skin and eyes called jaundice, abnormal blood tests, or loss of appetite. If these symptoms develop, the doctor will order more tests to determine their cause such as: chest

X-rays or ultrasounds; scans such as CT scans, PET scans, or bone scans; or possibly a biopsy of the area in question.

Once metastasis is confirmed, a course of treatment must be developed involving more chemo, radiation, surgery, or newer experimental therapies. This is something each patient must consider thoughtfully, and discuss thoroughly, with her doctor and her family, so that her needs and wishes are met. Family issues, financial matters, and personal feelings and attitudes all come in to play when considering how metastatic disease is going to be managed. Some women want aggressive treatment, despite the side effects it may cause. Others choose not to treat their disease aggressively, because they do not want to spend their days suffering from side effects. They may choose treatments that address only the symptoms of the disease, such as pain medications, steroids to reduce swelling, draining excess fluid from around the lungs to ease breathing, or medications to strengthen bones weakened by the cancer.

A Positive Outlook

Fighting breast cancer is an enormous struggle, and those who survive it often approach life with a different outlook. Robyn was thirty-six when she was diagnosed with Stage III breast cancer. "Cancer has made me stronger in so many ways," she says. "I have learned to not sweat the small stuff and try to always look at the big picture. It has made me realize how amazing my family and friends can be. The biggest life lesson that I have learned is to appreciate what you do have, take the time to smell the roses."[41]

New treatment methods for recurrent and metastatic breast cancer have greatly improved survival, and research continues at a fast pace. Living with breast cancer is not nearly as difficult as it once was, thanks to much improved knowledge, treatment methods, techniques for managing side effects, and greatly expanded sources of help and support. As Diane, a breast cancer survivor, says, "Cancer gives you a choice. Lay down and wait. Or get up and walk the dog."[42]

CHAPTER FIVE

The Future of Breast Cancer

Perhaps no other single disease has received as much attention, or been the focus of as much research, as breast cancer has in the last thirty years. Because of this explosion in awareness and knowledge, major advances have taken place in the areas of screening, diagnosing, treating, managing, and even preventing breast cancer. There is no doubt that breast cancer research has saved or improved the lives of countless women. Breast cancer still kills thousands of people around the world each year, however, so efforts continue on a grand scale. Many research projects are underway around the world in an effort to improve treatment and find new ways to treat, cure, and prevent breast cancer.

Clinical Trials

When a new treatment or procedure is first developed, it is tested in a laboratory on tissue samples or animals. These early tests are called preclinical trials. If the preclinical trials suggest that the new treatment might be safe and effective in people, clinical trials begin. Clinical trials are research projects that study how well the new treatment works on living human beings who have the disease or condition on which the treatment is designed to work. They are important because they establish whether or not the treatment is safe and effective in humans.

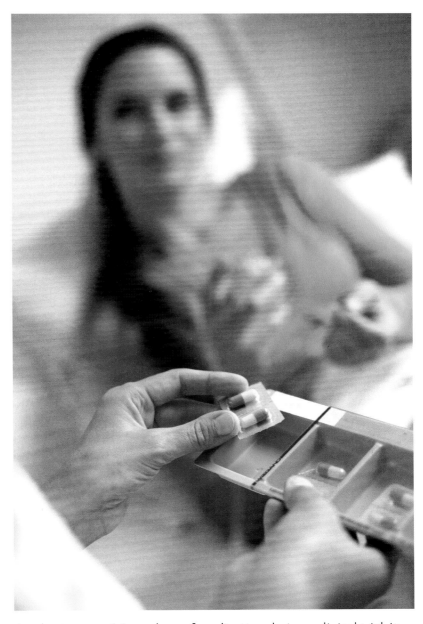

A volunteer receiving a dose of medication during a clinical trial. It takes many years for a medication to clear a clinical trial because researchers need to test the treatment on as many volunteers as possible to get the most accurate information.

It takes a long time for a drug or other treatment method to move from preclinical to clinical trials, and many do not ever get that far. The American Cancer Society estimates that only one out of a thousand new medicines makes it to clinical trials. Drugs that are currently used in breast cancer treatment have all been through years of preclinical trials, followed by several more years of clinical trials. It takes many years to complete a clinical trial because researchers need to test the treatment in as many human volunteers as possible, to get the most accurate information. They also need to study how the drug works over time, so they can get a clear picture of any long-term side effects the drug or treatment may have.

Clinical trials are usually done in four phases. Each phase builds upon the information learned during the previous phase. In Phase I trials, the goal is to determine if the treatment is safe for people. Since safety is unknown at this point, the test group is small, usually fewer than fifty people. Phase II focuses more on the most effective dose of the treatment, based on the information learned in Phase I. The study group will be larger in Phase II—about one hundred people. In Phase III, the new treatment is compared to treatments that already exist, to see if it is any better. Phase III may involve thousands of people and may collect data contributed by hospitals and other treatment centers all over the world. When Phase III is complete, it is time for the U.S. Food and Drug Administration (FDA) to consider its approval for the treatment. After FDA approval, the treatment may or may not enter a Phase IV. This phase looks at possible long-term effects of the treatment that may not show up during earlier phases. It also studies the possibility of other unexpected benefits the treatment may reveal over time.

Thousands of clinical trials are underway all over the world to find new and better ways to screen for, diagnose, treat, and manage breast cancer. The hope of these trials is to minimize the risk of getting breast cancer and to improve the survival of this disease. Other types of research studies, such as demographic studies that look at certain populations of people and

Vaccines for Breast Cancer

A vaccine is a drug that stimulates the body's immune system to recognize and attack invading disease organisms. Vaccines have been used for a very long time to prevent illnesses such as measles, polio, tetanus, and many others. Researchers have been working for decades to develop a vaccine that would stimulate the immune system to fight cancer cells and help prevent cancer from recurring after treatment—a technique called immunotherapy. Developing an effective cancer vaccine is very difficult because vaccines are usually made from foreign invaders such as bacteria or viruses, but cancer comes from the body's own cells. It is much more difficult to create a vaccine that will attack the body's own natural cells. Another stumbling block is that cancer tumors contain many different types of cancer cells, and a vaccine would be limited to attacking only the types it could recognize.

Research into breast cancer vaccines is looking at several ways to attack cancer cells. One approach is to develop drugs that mimic particular proteins that appear in cancer cells. The immune system would be stimulated to respond to the drug as if it were the cancer proteins and attack the cells that contain those proteins. Another approach is to develop drugs that attack only cells with specific cancer-causing genes, called oncogenes, in their DNA. Still another approach is to "tag" the cancer cell so that the immune system thinks it is a foreign substance and attacks it. Several cancer centers in the United States and other countries are preparing to begin clinical trials on these new approaches to fighting breast cancer.

their risk of disease, are also being conducted in the effort to learn as much as possible about breast cancer.

Learning More About Risk Factors

One very important step in conquering breast cancer is to learn more about who is at risk and what factors increase the risk, so that doctors and their patients can become better educated about how they can reduce their risk. Many research studies are finding that certain factors seem to increase risk, such as smoking, alcohol consumption, obesity, and certain environmental chemicals. Other studies are discovering what may decrease risk, such as regular physical exercise, Vitamin D, anti-inflammatory drugs including aspirin, and breastfeeding. Still others study substances such as caffeine, birth control pills, and fertility drugs, to determine what effect, if any, these substances have on breast cancer risk.

One of the most active areas of breast cancer research involves how lifestyle choices affect risk. This is important because lifestyle choices are something that people can control. Smoking is one lifestyle choice that has been linked to many different health problems, including breast cancer. Cigarette smoke contains dozens of different chemicals, many of which are very toxic to the human body and are capable of causing the genetic mutations that lead to the beginning of cancer growth.

One group of researchers at the University of Toronto conducted what is called a meta-analysis—they reviewed several recent studies that all focused on smoking and breast cancer. Dr. Neil Collishaw, the chairman of the group, says, "Until recently, evidence about the link between breast cancer and tobacco smoke, although voluminous, was inconclusive. But the panel's careful analysis of all available evidence, particularly recent evidence, led us to believe that there is persuasive evidence of risk."[43] The group found that the incidence of breast cancer is 20 percent higher in pre-menopausal women who smoke, especially when they start young, before they have children, when their breast tissue is not fully developed. Younger nonsmokers are also at increased risk even if they are only exposed to second-hand smoke. Risk is also increased in post-menopausal smokers. A 2008 study from Harvard University in Boston, Massachusetts, concluded that nicotine—an addictive substance in cigarette tobacco—even from second-hand smoke, can trigger both normal and cancerous breast tissue cells to grow and migrate—both within the breast and outside the breast. This study showed that nicotine exposure also increases the risk of developing a second breast cancer sometime in the future.

The Canadian study also confirmed a suspected link between smoking and the presence of a gene called NAT-2. This gene, found in 50 to 60 percent of the white population and 30 to 40 percent of African Americans, slows down the body's ability to get rid of a cancer-causing substance in cigarette smoke called aromatic amines. Long-term smokers with this gene have a 35 to 50 percent higher risk of breast cancer over nonsmokers. Other researchers have identified other genes, which may also play a role in increasing a person's risk of developing cancer. "We still know very little about what these genes do and how they might affect risk," says Dr. Christine B. Ambrosone of the Roswell Park Cancer Institute in Buffalo, New York. Studies such as these, further clarify the dangers of cigarette smoking and stress the need for programs to help people quit smoking. "We think the most important thing for people to do is to live a healthy lifestyle. Smoking cessation programs need to be further targeted to women as a means for preventing breast cancer. Here's one more adverse health outcome that smoking is likely related to."[44]

Another lifestyle factor that appears to have an impact on breast cancer risk is obesity. In 2001 researchers concluded that obesity and physical inactivity are related to an increased risk of several kinds of cancer, including breast cancer. Overweight, postmenopausal women have almost twice the risk of getting breast cancer as women of normal weight, and their risk of dying from breast cancer is also higher. Weight may also affect the type of breast cancer a woman develops. The very aggressive, inflammatory breast cancer is much more common in overweight women. "The more obese a patient is, the more aggressive the disease," says Dr. Massimo Cristofanilli of the M.D. Anderson Cancer Center in Houston, Texas. "We are learning that the fat tissue may increase inflammation that leads to more aggressive disease."[45]

Related to obesity is the impact that diet and exercise have on the survival of breast cancer. Several studies have looked at the impact of healthy diet or exercise in breast cancer survivors, as well as their ability to lower the risk of contracting breast cancer at all. A 2007 study looked at the effects on survival time of both diet and exercise together. "It looks like if you get your physical activity going and get your fruits and vegetables in [five or more servings], you can reduce your risk (of dying) significantly," says Dr. John Pierce, one of the researchers. The survival benefit was true even for obese women who adopted the healthier lifestyle. "Doing each alone didn't do it," Dr. Pierce says. "There was no benefit from each alone, but there was a benefit from both together."[46]

Studies such as these, and the Million Women Study, which, in 2001, demonstrated the significantly increased risk associated with alcohol consumption, and highlighted the importance of choosing a healthy lifestyle to aid in the prevention of breast cancer or increase survival in women who develop the disease. These are risk factors that can be controlled, and making the right choices can make a big difference.

Other Risk Factors

Scientists are studying many different factors to see what, if any, impact they may have on a woman's risk of developing breast cancer. For example, two studies from 2008 and 2009, done at the Fred Hutchinson Cancer Research Center in Seattle, Washington, found that the risk of getting breast cancer is 21 percent lower in premenopausal women who get migraine headaches and 26 percent lower in postmenopausal women who get these headaches, especially in decreasing the risk for hormone receptor-positive cancers. "It does appear that migraines may protect women from breast cancer, and that it's equally protective for both younger and older women,"[47] says Christopher Li, MD, PhD, the lead author of both studies. Since migraine headaches are linked with lowered estrogen levels, such as right before a menstrual period, doctors believe that the fluctuations

Some studies have found that women who get migraine headaches may be at a lower risk for developing breast cancer.

in estrogen levels that trigger migraine headaches may also account for the decreased risk of developing breast cancer.

Another factor being studied is the density of the breast tissue. Researchers at the Campbell Family Institute for Breast Cancer Research in Toronto, Canada, found that young women with denser breast tissue have a higher risk of breast cancer later in life. An additional finding was that taller women tended to have denser breast tissue. Connecting these two findings was that higher density of breast tissue is also linked to higher levels of growth hormones, which may explain the link between breast density and adult height. While more study is needed, this research suggests that measuring a young woman's breast tissue density may be a predictor of her future risk for breast cancer.

News About Screening

Research is underway to develop new and better methods of screening women for breast cancer. One experimental method being studied is molecular breast imaging (MBI), also called breast specific gamma imaging. Like other imaging studies, MBI uses a radioactive tracer, injected into the bloodstream. MBI appears to be beneficial for women with dense breast tissue that may hide a possible cancer on a regular mammogram. It is also much less expensive than an MRI. Dr. Deborah Rhodes of the Mayo Clinic helped develop MBI. "With MBI, a tumor is easy to see, even if it's in dense breast tissue,"[48] she says. Not only is MBI better able to detect breast cancers, it also yields fewer "false positives," which decreases the number of unnecessary breast biopsies.

The major drawback of MBI is that it uses a much higher dose of radiation than a mammogram, but the developers are working on that. "Our goal is to have a dose that's no higher than that from a routine mammogram," says Dr. Rhodes. "If we get results that are similar to, or better than, our last study, we'll be well on our way to supporting MBI as an option for women with dense breast tissue."[49]

Another screening test being studied is called digital tomosynthesis. Digital tomosynthesis uses X-rays, like a digital mammogram, but it creates a three-dimensional (3-D) view of the breast, rather than the two-dimensional image created by a mammogram. It takes images of the breast from at least eleven different angles, instead of the two that mammograms take. The test does not require uncomfortable compression of the breast, and it takes only seconds to complete. The images are sent to a computer for conversion into a 3-D image. Researchers are hopeful that digital tomosynthesis will help detect cancers in dense breast tissue, and that the improved comfort will lead more women to have regular screenings performed.

Ultrasound is a commonly used test that uses high-frequency sound waves to create an image of internal structures. Ultrasound is already being used to screen for breast cancer, but a newer method, called computed ultrasound risk evaluation, or CURE, sends the sound waves through water first. The patient lies on a table with an opening to fit the breast. A container under the hole holds warm water through which the sound waves are passed. The sound waves are reflected off the tissue and sent back to a computer, which converts them into images. "So far it's been able to see almost all the cancers that are above five millimeters [one fifth of an inch]," says Peter Littrup, MD, radiologist at Karmanos Cancer Institute in Detroit, Michigan. "We can get images with a lot more information than we've currently been able to. In fact we're trying to also use this to reduce unnecessary biopsies."[50] Judy, a breast cancer survivor who has had a recurrence, is involved in a CURE trial. "It feels like a little sauna on your breast," she says. "The water temperature is warm, it's very relaxing, it's comforting,"[51]

Genetics and Breast Cancer Treatment

The field of genetics has provided an entirely new way of approaching breast cancer and its treatment. With the discovery of the BRCA gene mutations, the HER-2 gene, and others, the door was opened to new ways to fight the disease. Discoveries in genetics continue to help doctors refine treatment plans to make them less uncomfortable, more effective, and more individualized for each patient.

In 2007 researchers at several places around the world discovered genetic mutations in several genes that are common in people with breast cancer. For example, scientists at Harvard University and at the National Cancer Institute found four mutations in a gene called FGFR2 in postmenopausal women with breast cancer. The mutations raise the risk of breast cancer by up to 60 percent if the person has two copies of this mutation. They found that up to 60 percent of women may carry at least one of the four mutations in this gene. Researchers at centers in Great Britain and the Netherlands have found mutations in three other genes that were also common in breast cancer patients.

A group of researchers at Princeton University have identified a gene called MTDH that makes a cancer more likely to metastasize, and makes it more resistant to chemotherapy. When tumor cells were implanted in mice, those with an active form of this gene spread seven times more than tumors with an inactive form. "Inhibiting this gene in breast cancer patients

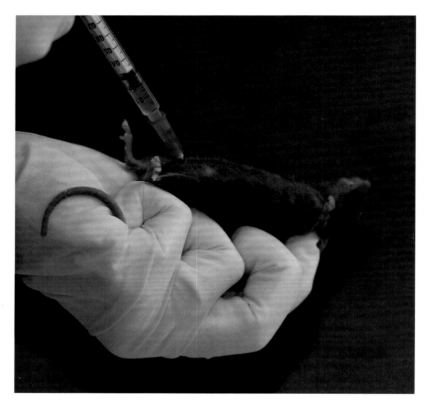

Researchers at Princeton University have found that when they injected mice with tumor cells that had the active form of the gene MTDH the tumors spread seven times more than tumors with an inactive form of the gene.

will achieve two important goals: reduce the chance of recurrence, and decrease the risk of metastatic dissemination," says Dr. Yibin Kang, PhD, one of the researchers. "These are the two main reasons why breast cancer patients die from the disease."[52]

On the other hand, scientists are also discovering genes that help stop cancer from metastasizing. For example, in October 2009, researchers at the Wistar Institute in Philadelphia, Pennsylvania, published research in which they identified a gene called KLF17, which can accurately predict whether a breast cancer will spread to the lymph nodes. The researchers took cancer cells in which the KLF17 gene had been "knocked down," or suppressed, and other cells in which the gene was still active, and injected them into mice. Within weeks, the mice with the knocked down cells developed lung metastases, and those with the active KLF17 gene did not. "Identifying the gene that suppresses the spread of tumor cells and the mechanisms by which this suppression occurs can lead to the discovery of new markers of metastasis and potential targets for cancer prevention and treatment,"[53] says Qihong Huang, MD, PhD, assistant professor at The Wistar Institute and senior author of the study.

Genetic Tests on Cancer Tissue

Two new tests, done on the cancer tissue itself, help determine the genetic make-up of cancer cells. The Spot-Light HER2 CISH test was approved for use in 2008. It determines whether a breast tumor is HER-2 positive or negative. It is important to know this because HER-2 positive cancers are especially aggressive and fast-growing. They also tend to be hormone receptor-negative, so they will not respond well to hormone therapy. They do, however, respond to a drug called Herceptin, which blocks the message to grow and divide that the HER-2 protein sends to the cell. The test uses a special stain, which is applied to the tumor tissue and colors the HER-2 genes. This shows how many copies of the gene there are in the tumor cells. The more copies of the gene there are, the more HER-2 protein will be present on the surface of the cell.

Another new test done on cancer tissue is called the Onco-type DX test. This test is done on breast tumors that are early stage, ER positive, and lymph node-negative—cancers which will respond to hormone therapy and which have not spread outside the breast. These cancers have a very low risk of recurring, but a small number of them do still recur after treatment. This test helps determine if the patient's cancer is one that has a higher than normal risk of recurrence. It also helps a doctor decide whether or not his patient needs chemotherapy, as well as hormone therapy, to reduce the risk of recurrence.

Cancer Stem Cells

The traditional approach to treating cancer has been to kill as many cells in the tumor as possible. New research, being done in several centers around the world, is now suggesting that this may not be as effective in preventing recurrences of cancer because the wrong cells are being targeted. The research has identified certain kinds of cancer cells, called cancer stem cells, which may be responsible for creating all the other cancer cells in a tumor and for creating new cancers.

Stem cells are immature cells that have not yet differentiated into any particular kind of cell. Cancer stem cells not only reproduce themselves, they can also become other types of cancer cells within the same tumor. Research at the University of Michigan showed that as few as one hundred to two hundred of these stem cells, injected into mice, were capable of starting new tumors, while thousands of other tumor cells from the same tumor did not. The research has also shown that cancer stem cells are particularly difficult to kill, which may explain why some cancers recur even after aggressive treatment. The research suggests that drugs need to be developed that will target cancer stem cells and eliminate them, thereby eliminating their opportunity to create new cancers.

The Oncotype DX is a genomic test, which means that, unlike a genetic test, which looks for inherited genetic mutations, it examines a group of twenty-one different genes and their activity in the cancer cell. It gives the tumor its own genetic "personality," in the form of a recurrence score. A score less than eighteen indicates a low risk of recurrence, from eighteen to thirty-one is considered intermediate, and a score more than thirty-one indicates a high risk. When combined with other information about the tumor, the doctor and his patient can make a more informed decision about whether the benefit of chemotherapy would outweigh the side effects. Currently, a clinical trial called the TAILORx trial (Trial Assigning Individualized Options for Treatment), sponsored by the National Cancer Institute, is underway to help define treatment recommendations for women who fall into the intermediate range on the Oncotype DX.

Targeted Therapies

Discovering more about the role of genetics in breast cancer has led to the development of more advanced methods of therapy called targeted, or biological, therapies. Whenever a unique characteristic of a cancer is identified, such as a gene, a protein, or a unique cellular process, drugs can be developed that treat that characteristic as a target and interfere with that particular characteristic. They can tell a particular gene or a protein what to do to stop cancer growth. Targeted therapies specifically target only cancer cells, their genes, and the proteins they make. They do not harm normal, healthy cells, so their side effects tend to be milder than traditional chemotherapy. At this time, targeted therapies are being used along with traditional chemotherapies.

One of the first targeted therapies to be FDA approved was Herceptin, which was first approved for use in breast cancer treatment in 1998. Since then, trials have been conducted to evaluate its effectiveness when used along with other treatments, as well as to establish the most beneficial length of time

Herceptin became one of the first targeted therapy drugs for cancer when it was approved by the FDA in 1998.

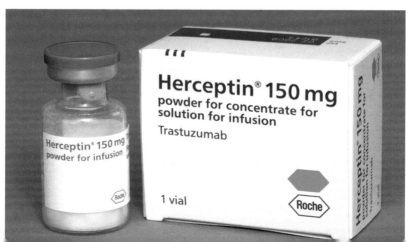

for treatment. Herceptin is a kind of drug called a monoclonal antibody—a synthetic, or man-made, version of an immune system protein. Herceptin specifically targets HER-2 positive cancers, attaching itself to the HER-2 protein and interfering with its growth signals to the cell. It may also help stimulate the immune system and help it attack cancer cells. Another kind of targeted therapy works by interfering with angiogenesis—the growth of new blood vessels that supply the tumor cells. Avastin is the most commonly used drug in this category. Its target is a protein called vascular endothelial growth factor (VEGF). Tumor cells can secrete VEGF to stimulate angiogenesis. Avastin binds itself to VEGF and prevents it from stimulating new blood vessels. Without a blood supply of its own, tumor growth slows or even stops.

A brand new and very promising class of targeted therapy drugs is the poly ADP-ribose polymerase (PARP) inhibitors. PARP is a protein that repairs damage in the DNA of cancer cells. If a cancer cell's DNA has been damaged by radiation or chemo, for example, the PARP protein can fix it, making the treatment less effective. PARP inhibitors interfere with PARP's ability to repair damaged DNA. Early research into PARP inhibitors is exciting for several reasons. They appear to be effective in patients with the BRCA-1 and BRCA-2 mutations, even to the point of preventing breast cancer from even starting in women who have inherited these mutations. They also appear to be effective for treating the very difficult triple-negative form of breast cancer. They may also be useful for other types of cancer, such as brain and uterine cancers. They do not affect healthy cells at all, only cancer cells.

Research is showing that attacking breast cancer at the level of its DNA may be the core of breast cancer treatment in the future. Promising new targeted therapies are being developed and perfected that will be highly effective and very selective, improving survival and minimizing side effects.

Notes

Introduction: A Sisterhood of Struggle and Strength

1. Christa, "Christa's Story." BreastCancerStories.org, May 10, 2006. www.breastcancerstories.org/chapter/270.
2. Quoted in Cordelia S. Bland, "The Halsted Mastectomy: Present Illness and Past History," *Western Journal of Medicine*, June 1981, p. 549.
3. Quoted in Greg Botelho, "Breast Cancer: The Path Traveled and the Road aAhead," CNN.com, October 11, 2005. www.cnn.com/2005/HEALTH/02/22/breast.cancer/index.html.
4. Quoted in Deborah Axelrod, Rosie O'Donnell and Tracy Chutorian Semler, *Bosom Buddies: Lessons and Laughter on Breast Cancer*. New York: Warner Books, 1999, p.1.
5. Quoted in Axelrod, O'Donnell, and Semler, *Bosom Buddies*, p.1.
6. Quoted in Botelho, "Breast Cancer," CNN.com.
7. Quoted in Botelho, "Breast Cancer," CNN.com.

Chapter One: What Is Breast Cancer?

8. Rosalind Benedet, NP and Mark C. Rounsaville, MD, *Understanding Lumpectomy—A Treatment Guide for Breast Cancer*. Omaha, NE: Addicus Books, 2004, p.4.
9. Yashar Hirshaut, MD and Peter I. Pressman, MD, *Breast Cancer, The Complete Guide*, 5th ed. New York: Bantam Dell, 2008, p. 40.
10. Quoted in Julie Steenhuysen, "Scientists Discover How BRCA-1 Gene Causes Cancer." Reuters, December 9, 2007. http://www.reuters.com/article/healthNews/idUSN0935659520071209.

11. Rosy Daniel, *The Cancer Prevention Book—A Complete Mind/Body Approach to Stopping Cancer Before It Starts*. Alameda, CA: Hunter House, 2002, p.1.
12. Quoted in Suzanne W. Braddock, MD, Jane M. Kercher, MD, John J. Edney, MD, and Melanie Morrissey Clark, *Straight Talk About Breast Cancer*. Omaha, NE: Addicus Books, 2002, p.22.

Chapter Two: Symptoms and Diagnosis

13. James Thompson, "Men get breast cancer, too!" Breast-CancerStories.org, March 2, 2004. www.breastcancer stories.org/chapter/71.
14. Patsy Hays, "Standing Up to Cancer." TODAY on msnbc .com, October 23, 2009. http://www.reuters.com/article/healthNews/idUSN0935659520071209.
15. Quoted in Breastcancer.org, "Breast Cancer Tests: Screening, Diagnosis, and Monitoring." www.breast cancer.org/symptoms/testing/types/.
16. Quoted in Breastcancer.org, "Mammograms." www .breastcancer.org/symptoms/testing/types/mammograms
17. Quoted in Breastcancer.org, "Mammography: Benefits, Risks, What You Need to Know." http://www.breast cancer.org/symptoms/testing/types/mammograms/benefits_risks.jsp.
18. Quoted in Breastcancer.org, "Diagnostic vs Screening Mammograms?" www.breastcancer.org/symptoms/testing/types/mammograms/benefits_risks.jsp.
19. Quoted in Rachel A. Clark, MS, Suzanne Snedeker, PhD, and Carol Devine, PhD, "Estrogen and Breast Cancer Risk: The Relationship." Cornell University Program on Breast Cancer and Environmental Risk Factors, March 1998, updated August 16, 2001. http://envirocancer .cornell.edu/FactSheet/General/fs9.estrogen.cfm.

Chapter Three: Treatment of Breast Cancer

20. Pat Kelly and Mark Levine, MD, *Breast Cancer: The Facts You Need to Know About Diagnosis, Treatment, and Beyond*. Buffalo, NY: Firefly Books, 2002, p.30.
21. Breastcancer.org, "Treatment and Side Effects." www .breastcancer.org/treatment/.

22. Quoted in Breastcancer.org, "Stages of Breast Cancer." www.breastcancer.org/symptoms/diagnosis/staging.jsp.
23. Nancy, "Nancy's Story." BreastCancerStories.org, October 10, 2008. http://www.breastcancerstories.org/chapter/260.
24. "Nancy's Story."
25. Quoted in Breastcancer.org, "How Radiation Works." www.breastcancer.org/treatment/radiation/how_works.jsp.
26. Wendy, "Wendy's Story." BreastCancerStories.org, July 25, 2004. www.breastcancerstories.org/chapter/1221.
27. Jeannette, "Jeannette's Story." BreastCancerStories.org, January 9, 2008. www.breastcancerstories.org/chapter/153.

Chapter Four: Living With Breast Cancer

28. Quoted in "Knowledge is Key, Says Breast Cancer Survivor." American Cancer Society, Coping With Physical and Emotional Changes, April 13, 2009. http://www.cancer.org/docroot/FPS/content/FPS_1_Knowledge_is_Key_Says_Survivor_Rita_Gore.asp.
29. Quoted in Rick Allen, "Breast Cancer Patients' Husbands Find Strength." *The Gainesville Sun*, Gainesville.com, October 24, 2009. http://www.gainesville.com/article/20091024/ARTICLES/910239942/1004/LIVING?Title=Breast-cancer-patients-husbands-find-strength.
30. Quoted in Breastcancer.org, "Is Mastectomy Right for You?" www.breastcancer.org/treatment/surgery/mastectomy/who_for.jsp.
31. Wendy, "Wendy's Story," BreastCancerStories.org, February 25, 2004. www.breastcancerstories.org/chapter/69
32. Quoted in Breastcancer.org, "Chemotherapy Side Effects." www.breastcancer.org/treatment/chemotherapy/side_effects.jsp.
33. Quoted in Samantha Critchell, "Campaign Aids Cancer Patient Beauty Routine." *Springfield News-Leader*, October 16, 2009, p.4C.
34. Quoted in Critchell, "Campaign Aids Breast Cancer Patient Beauty Routine."
35. Transcribed from interview with Hoda Kotb and Kathie Lee Gifford, *Today Show*, October 16, 2009.

36. Transcribed from interview with Hoda Kotb and Kathie Lee Gifford, *Today Show*, October 16, 2009.

37. Quoted in Breastcancer.org, "Your Response to Treatment." www.breastcancer.org/symptoms/type/recur_metast/living_metast/treat_response.jsp.

38. Quoted in Breastcancer.org, "Getting the Support You Need." www.breastcancer.org/symptoms/types/recur_metast/living_metast/support.jsp.

39. Quoted in Breastcancer.org, "When Breast Cancer Might Come Back and How to Detect It." www.breastcancer.org/symptopms/type/recur_metast/where_recur/.

40. Quoted in Breastcancer.org, "If Cancer Comes Back." www.breastcancer.org/symptoms/type/recur_metast/fear_combk.jsp.

41. Robyn Wolfe, "Standing Up To Cancer." TODAY on msnbc.com http://www.msnbc.msn.com/id/33245310.

42. Diane Slomowitz, "Standing Up To Cancer."

Chapter Five: The Future of Breast Cancer

43. Quoted in Kristina Fiore, "Smoking Causes Breast Cancer, Analysis Shows." MedPage Today, April 24, 2009. http://www.medpagetoday.com/PrimaryCare/Smoking/13899.

44. Quoted in Anne Harding, "Common Gene Boosts Breast Cancer Risk in Smokers." http://www.breastcancer.org/risk/new_research/20080214.jsp.

45. Quoted in "Locally Advanced Breast Cancer More Deadly in Obese." Caring4Cancer, March 14, 2008. http://www.caring4cancer.com/go/multiplemyeloma/news?NewsItemId=20080314elin013.xml.

46. Quoted in Charnicia Huggins, "Diet Plus Exercise Up Survival After Cancer." Reuters Health, June 21, 2007. http://www.reuters.com/article/healthNews/idUSCOL15786220070621.

47. Quoted in Kathleen Doheny, "Migraines Linked to Lower Breast Cancer Risk." WebMD, July 9, 2009. http://www.webmd.com/migraines-headaches/news/20090709/migraines-linked-lower-breast-cancer-risk.

48. Quoted in Mayo Clinic, "Molecular Breast Imaging: A Better Way to Spot Tumors in Dense Breast Tissue." Mayo

Clinic news release, March 10, 2009. http://www
.mayoclinic.org/news2009-mchi/5203.html.

49. Mayo Clinic, "Molecular Breast Imaging."
50. Quoted in "Sound Detects Breast Cancer." *Science Daily*, August 1, 2008. http://www.sciencedaily.com/ videos/2008/0810-sound_detects_breast_cancer.htm.
51. Quoted in "Sound Detects Breast Cancer."
52. Quoted in Charles Bankhead, "Breast Cancer Metastasis Gene Identified." MedPage Today, January 5, 2009. http:// www.medpagetoday.com/HematologyOncology/Breast Cancer/12330.
53. Quoted in "Gene That Regulates Breast Cancer Metastasis Identified." *Science Daily*, October 7, 2009. http:// www.sciencedaily.com/releases/2009/10/091005161322. htm.

Glossary

alopecia: The loss of hair, especially from the head.

anemia: A blood disorder in which red blood cells are too low, causing fatigue and weakness.

angiogenesis: The process whereby a tumor creates new blood vessels for itself.

apoptosis: The normal process of cell division, growth, and natural death.

axilla: The armpit.

axillary node dissection: A surgical procedure in which the lymph nodes are removed from the axilla.

benign: A term that describes a harmless tumor that does not spread to other organs.

bilateral mastectomy: The surgical removal of both breasts.

biopsy: The removal of tissue for examination to arrive at a diagnosis.

bone scan: A diagnostic test in which a radioactive tracer is injected and taken up by bone tissue; done to identify possible areas of cancer metastasis.

brachytherapy: A precise method of administering radiation directly to the site of a cancer from inside the body.

BRCA gene: A gene which plays a role in cell division; mutations in the BRCA gene are a risk factor for breast cancer.

cachexia: A condition of physical "wasting away" characterized by severe weight loss and weakness.

carcinoma: Cancer that comes from skin, glands, or the lining of internal organs.

chemotherapy: Also referred to as "chemo"; the treatment of cancer using drugs that kill cancer cells.

computed ultrasound risk evaluation (CURE): A promising new diagnostic method that uses ultrasound waves and computers to screen for breast cancer.

clinical trial: A research study that looks at how a particular treatment works in human beings.

core biopsy: A method of obtaining tissue cells for microscopic examination using a hollow needle.

CT (computed tomography) scan: A test that uses X-ray to make detailed pictures of structures inside the body.

digital tomosynthesis: A diagnostic test which uses X-ray to create a three-dimensional view of the breast.

ducts: The tiny tubes inside the breast that carry milk to the nipple.

estrogen: A hormone that has several functions related to sexual development of the female.

false-positive: A test result that comes back as positive, but is eventually found to be negative.

genetic marker: A gene that, if present in a cell, can indicate specific characteristics of the cell. This information helps doctors decide upon a treatment plan for breast cancer.

HER-2: A protein molecule that is responsible for cell growth and division; too much HER-2 can cause cells to grow abnormally fast.

hormone receptor: A specialized molecule on the surface of hormone target organs that binds to the hormone molecule and carries it into the nucleus of the cell, which allows the cell to respond to the hormone.

hormone therapy: A method of cancer treatment that interferes with the ability of estrogen to support cancer growth.

immunotherapy: Cancer treatment that stimulates the body's own immune system to fight against cancer cells.

in situ: A Latin phrase that means "in place."

latissimus dorsi flap: A method of reconstructive breast surgery that uses the latissimus dorsi muscle from the back to replace the breast.

lobules: Collections of tiny sacs inside the breast that produce and secrete milk.

lumpectomy: A surgical procedure in which only the area of the cancerous tumor is removed, rather than the whole breast.

lymphedema: Swelling of the arm caused by removal of the lymph nodes in the armpit.

lymph nodes: Small bean-shaped structures located throughout the body that collect and concentrate unwanted substances so that immune system cells can eliminate them from the body.

margins: The edges or ends of a piece of tissue that have been surgically removed; the margins are checked for cancer cells to make sure that all the cancer has been removed.

malignant: A term that describes harmful, cancerous tumors that can spread to other parts of the body.

mammogram: An X-ray test that is used to screen women for breast cancer.

mastectomy: The surgical removal of the breast.

metastasis: The spread of cancer from its original location to other organs.

metastatic: A cancerous tumor that has grown in a part of the body other than where it started.

molecular breast imaging (MBI): A new method of breast imaging that uses radioactive substances to detect cancer and may be more helpful than mammograms for women with dense breast tissue.

monoclonal antibody: Man-made immune system antibodies that can be used to target very specific types of cells, such as cancer cells, and stimulate an immune response to destroy those cells.

MRI (magnetic resonance imaging): A diagnostic test that uses radio waves and magnets to produce cross-sectional images of structures in the body.

mutation: A change, or error, in a gene that cause it to malfunction.

needle aspiration: A method of obtaining tissue cells for microscopic examination using a needle and syringe to withdraw the cells.

neutropenia: A blood condition in which white blood cells are abnormally low, making a person more vulnerable to getting infections.

oncogenes: Genes which, when they mutate, make it easier for a cell to become cancerous.

oncology/oncologist: The study of cancer, its causes, diagnosis, and treatments. An oncologist is a physician who specializes in oncology.

oncotype DX test: A test done on cancer tissue cells that examines a group of twenty-one different genes and their activity in the cancer cell.

palpation/palpable: A method of identifying potential problems in a body part using gentle pressure with the hands; a mass that can be felt with the fingers is said to be a palpable mass.

peau d'orange: A French phrase meaning "skin of an orange"; a skin condition in which the skin has a thickened, puckered appearance like the skin of an orange.

PET (positron emission tomography) scan: A diagnostic test that uses radioactive substances along with normal body functions such as sugar metabolism to locate areas of cancer.

prophylactic mastectomy: The surgical removal of a healthy breast in order to prevent it from developing cancer.

radiation therapy: A method of cancer treatment that uses radiation to interfere with the ability of cancer cells to reproduce.

sentinel node biopsy: A surgical procedure in which an axillary lymph node is examined for cancer cells to see if the cancer has spread outside the breast.

spot-light HER2 CISH test: A tissue test that determines if a tumor is HER-2 positive or negative.

stem cells: Immature cells that have not yet specialized into any particular type of cell.

surgical biopsy: A surgical procedure in which a sample of tissue is removed and examined for the presence of cancer.

targeted therapy: A precise method of cancer treatment that uses drugs designed to target only cancer cells and not healthy cells.

thrombocytopenia: A blood condition in which platelets are abnormally low, making a person more susceptible to prolonged bleeding.

TRAM flap: A method of reconstructive breast surgery that uses a portion of the rectus abdominis muscle from the lower abdomen to replace the breast.

tumor: An abnormal growth of cells that creates a mass, or lump, in the body.

tumor burden: The total amount of tumor tissue in a person; the higher the tumor burden, the more energy and nutrients it takes from healthy cells.

ultrasound: A diagnostic test that uses high-frequency sound waves to create an image on a screen of structures inside the body.

Organizations to Contact

American Breast Cancer Foundation (ABCF)
1220 B East Joppa Rd., Ste. 332
Baltimore, MD 21286
1-410-825-9338
www.abcf.org
e-mail: contactABCF@abcf.org

The mission of the ABCF is to provide education, emotional and financial support, and early detection screening services to those in low-income, rural communities in the United States.

American Cancer Society (ACS)
250 Williams St., Ste. 600
Atlanta, GA 30329
1-800-ACS-2345
www.cancer.org

The ACS works for cancer treatment, prevention, and quality of life issues through research, education, patient services, and rehabilitation. Their Web site features news and information, message boards, links to their programs (including Reach To Recovery), and chat rooms.

Breast Cancer Network of Strength (formerly Y-ME National Breast Cancer Organization)
135 S. LaSalle St., Ste. 2000
Chicago, IL 60603
1-312-986-8338, or 24-hour hotline 1-800-221-2141
www.networkofstrength.org

Founded in 1978, Y-Me started with twelve women and has grown into a national organization with chapters nationwide. Its goal is to decrease the impact of breast cancer on women and families by providing information, increasing awareness, and helping ensure that no woman has to face breast cancer alone.

Cancer Care, Inc.
275 Seventh Ave., Fl. 22
New York, NY 10001
1-800-813-HOPE
www.cancercare.org
e-mail: info@cancercare.org

Cancer Care offers education, emotional support, information, and practical help to people with cancer and their families. Specialists are available for personal phone consultations.

National Breast Cancer Coalition (NBCC)
1101 Seventeenth St. NW, Ste. 1300
Washington, DC 20036
1-800-622-2838
www.stopbreastcancer.org

The NBCC works to promote increased funding for breast cancer research at national, state, and local levels and works with scientists to improve diagnosis, treatment, and access to high-quality care.

National Cancer Institute (NCI)
31 Center Dr.
Bethesda, MD 20892
1-800-4CANCER
www.cancer.gov
e-mail: cancergovstaff@mail.nih.gov

The NCI is part of the National Institutes of Health (NIH). It is the federal government's principle agency for cancer research and training. It conducts its own research, as well as supports research done in other institutions, and collects and distributes cancer information.

The Susan G. Komen Breast Cancer Foundation
5005 LBJ Fwy., Ste. 250
Dallas, TX 75244
1-877-GOKOMEN
www.komen.org or www.breastcancerinfo.com

Founded by Nancy Brinker to honor her sister, Susan G. Komen, who died of breast cancer in 1980, this nonprofit organization works through a large network of volunteers in local chapters throughout the United States. Its mission is to eliminate breast cancer as a life-threatening disease through research, education, screening, and treatment.

For More Information

Books

Suzanne W. Braddock, MD, Jane M. Kercher, MD, John J. Edney, MD, and Melanie Morissey Clark, *Straight Talk About Breast Cancer—From Diagnosis to Recovery*. Omaha, NE: Addicus Books, 2002. A well-written, clear and concise, and illustrated book about all aspects of cancer.

Janet Majure, *Breast Cancer*. Berkeley Heights, NJ: Enslow, 2000. Discusses the history, diagnosis, prevention, and treatments of breast cancer and explores its effects on society.

Terry L. Smith, *Breast Cancer: Current and Emerging Trends in Detection and Treatment*. New York, NY: Rosen Central, 2005. Includes stories from well-known survivors of breast cancer and provides general information on anatomy, diagnosis, treatment, and coping, and future trends

Ann Speltz, *The Year My Mother Was Bald*. Washington, DC: Magination Press, 2003. A girl keeps a journal about her mother's fight with breast cancer. Includes a list of resources.

Carol G. Vogel, *Breast Cancer: Questions and Answers for Young Women*. Breckenridge, CO: Twenty-first Century Books, 2001. Written in question-and-answer format, this updated version of an earlier book includes advances in breast cancer research, diagnosis, and treatment.

Marisa C. Weiss and Isabel Friedman, *Taking Care of Your "Girls": A Breast Health Guide for Girls, Teens, and In-betweens*. New York, NY: Three Rivers Press, 2008. A book for young girls about their breasts—development, self-image, clothing, and breast health.

Internet Sources

Breast Cancer Fund, "Questions and Answers About Breast Cancer for School-age Children." http://www.breastcancer fund.org/site/c.kwKXLdPaE/b.84637/k.440B/Questions_ and_Answers_for_Children.htm. Question-and-answer format about breast cancer for younger children.

Center for Young Women's Health, "Breast Health: a Guide for Teens."http://www.youngwomenshealth.org/breast_health .html. Information for teenage girls about breast health and development.

KidsHealth, "Breast Cancer."http://kidshealth.org/kid/grownup/ conditions/breast_cancer.html. A Web site for children about breast cancer.

MayoClinic.com, "Breast Cancer." http://www.mayoclinic.com/ health/breast-cancer/DS00328. An overview of breast cancer from one of the nation's leading health care centers.

TeensHealth, "How to Perform a Breast Self-Examination." http://kidshealth.org/teen/sexual_health/girls/bse.html. An educational page for teenage girls about the very important routine of breast self-exams.

Web sites

Breastcancer.org (www.breastcancer.org) An extremely comprehensive site offering a wealth of information on all aspects of breast cancer.

National Breast Cancer Foundation, Inc. (www.national breastcancer.org) Provides information and help for those coping with breast cancer.

Susan G. Komen for the Cure (http://ww5.komen.org) Provides information about the Susan G. Komen Foundation and has a link to "Understanding Breast Cancer."

Index

Medical treatments as risk
factor, 27–28, 29–30
Medullary carcinoma, 20–21
Men
deaths, 9
risk, 25
Menopause, drug-induced, 75
Menstruation as risk factor, 27
Meta-analysis, 86
Metastasis
explained, 16–17
KLF17 gene as predictor of,
92–93
monitoring tests and, 45
MTDH gene and, 91–92
as recurrence, 80–81
sentinel nodes and, 55–56
stages and, 23
Metastatic breast cancer,
80–81
Methotrexate, 57, 75
Migraine headaches, 88–89
Million Women Study, 28–29,
88
Molecular breast imaging
(MBI), 89–90
Monitoring tests, 33–34,
44–47, *45*
Monoclonal antibodies, 96
MRI (magnetic resonance
imaging), 39, 46
MTDH gene, 91–92

N
NAT-2 gene, 87
Native American women,
incidence and death rates, 9
Nausea, 71, 72–73
Navigators (radiation
detection machines), 54–55
Needle aspiration biopsies,
40, *40*
Needle localization, 41

Neutropenia, 74
Nipple, Paget's disease of the,
21
Nipple discharge, 33
Noninvasive cancers, *79*
stage, 23
treatment, 51, 58
types, 20

O
Obesity as risk factor, 29, 87
Oncogenes, 85
Oncotype DX test, 93
Orel, Susan G., 33, 34

P
Paget's disease of the nipple, 21
Palpation, 37
Parsons, Ramon, 27
Partial breast radiation, 63–64
Peau d'orange, 21
PET (positive emission
tomography) scans, 46–47
Physical activity
after surgery, 69, 72
risk and, 29, 88
Physical therapy, 69
Pierce, John, 88
Plant alkaloids, 57
Poly ADP-ribose polymerase
(PARP) inhibitors, 96
PR-positive tumors, 43, 59
Pre-cancerous conditions, 20
Pregnancy as risk factor, 27
Pressman, Peter I., 21
Previous breast cancer as risk
factor, 27
Progesterone and HRT, 29–30
Progesterone receptors, 42,
43, 59
Prognosis
importance of staging for,
21–22

Cancer Foundation, 31
Symptoms, early, 31–33, *32*

T
TAILORx trial (Trial
   Assigning Individualized
   Options for Treatment), 95
Tamoxifen, 59, *60*
Targeted therapies, 93, *95*,
   95–96
Tissue flap reconstructions,
   68–69
TRAM (transverse rectus
   abdominis muscle) flaps,
   68–69
Treatment therapies
   anti-estrogen hormone
      therapy, 44
   chemotherapy, 51, 56–59,
      71–76
   complementary, 54–55
   genetic tests and, 93–95
   HER-2 status and, 93
   hormone, 58–59, *60*
   MTDH gene and, 91–92
   patient's role, 64
   planning, 49
   radiation, 51, 61–64, *62*
   reason for combination of
      methods, 48
   research in genetic, 91–93
   See also specific types of
      surgery
Triple-negative breast
   cancers, 44, 96

Tube and button
   brachytherapy, 63–64
Tumor burden, 17–18
Tumors
   benign, 14–16
   cancerous, 16–18
   development of, 14, 43
   margins, 41, 50
Types of breast cancer, 19–21,
   93

U
Ultrasound, *38*, 38–39
U.S. Food and Drug
   Administration (FDA), 84

V
Vaccines, 85
Vascular endothelial growth
   factor (VEGF), 44, 96
Visco, Fran, 13
Vital organs, cancer spread
   to, 17
Vomiting, 71, 72–73

W
Weight lifting, 72
Weiss, Marisa, 49, 61
Women, deaths, 9

X
X-rays, 46

Y
Yoga, 55

Picture Credits

About the Author

Lizabeth Hardman received her Bachelor of Science in Nursing from the University of Florida in 1978, and her Bachelor of Science in Secondary Education from Southwest Missouri State University in 1991. She currently works as a surgical nurse.

Ms. Hardman has published both fiction and nonfiction for children and adults, and especially enjoys writing about medicine and history. She lives in Springfield, Missouri, with her two daughters, Rebecca and Wendy; two dogs; two cats; and two birds. When she is not working or writing, she enjoys reading, hiking, St. Louis Cardinals baseball and Florida Gators football.